*In memory of
Leann Anderson,
whose wit, talent, generosity
and knowledge continues to
inspire us all.*

303 Marketing Tips

Guaranteed to Boost Your Business

Current titles from Entrepreneur Media Inc.:

Start Your Own Business:
The Only Start-up Book You'll Ever Need

Young Millionaires: Inspiring Stories to
Ignite Your Entrepreneurial Dreams

Forthcoming titles from Entrepreneur Media Inc.:

Business Plans Made Easy:
It's Not as Hard as You Think

Where's the Money? Sure-fire financial Solutions
for Your Small Business

Knockout Marketing: Powerful Strategies
to Punch Up Your Sales

Entrepreneur MAGAZINE'S

303 Marketing Tips

Guaranteed to Boost Your Business

Managing Editor: Marla Markman
Copy Editor: Marisa Laudadio
Layout Design: Sylvia H. Lee
Proofreader: Mandy Erickson
Production Company: Coghill Composition Company
Cover Design: Barry Littmann
Indexer: Alta Indexing Service

Library of Congress Cataloging-in-Publication Data
303 marketing tips: guaranteed to boost your business / by Rieva Lesonsky, editorial
director, Entrepreneur Magazine, and Leann Anderson.

     p.   cm.
    Includes index.
    ISBN 1-891984-02-0
    1. Marketing. 2. Marketing—Management. 3. Consumer behavior.
  I. Lesonsky, Rieva. II. Anderson, Leann II. Entrepreneur (Irvine, Calif.)
  III. Title: Three hundred three marketing tips. IV. Title: Marketing Tips
  HF5415.A15   1999
  658.8—dc21   98-41359
                                                      CIP

Printed in the United States of America

09 08 07 06 05 04 03 02 01 00   10 9 8 7 6 5 4 3 2 1

Table Of Contents

Introduction

Several years ago, I got a call from a gentleman who owned a number of jewelry stores. He said he wanted some help with marketing. He told me he had run out of ideas for ads and just couldn't come up with something fresh. Could I see to it that some new ads were created before the holidays rolled around?

What's wrong with this request? Well, nothing, if you don't mind pouring money down the drain. You see, this individual suffered from the same malady as countless other people engaged in small-business ventures. He confused advertising with marketing.

While advertising is an important part of the marketing mix, it's only one element. Marketing encompasses a number of factors and has to be consistent, comprehensive and customized to your particular situation. The terrific thing about knowing this little kernel of truth is it allows you to take advantage of a whole bevy of marketing opportunities and doesn't lock you into the challenge of only generating something fresh for your advertisements.

Making the most of all these opportunities is

what this book is about. It will help you see new ways to tell and sell. It will bring into focus the importance of knowing your customers, the tried-and-true methods of promoting your business or product, and the tremendous value of thinking creatively when trying to get a leg up on the competition.

From garnering more and better publicity to discovering ways to harness the power of the Internet, *303 Marketing Tips* will present you with options and ideas that may never have occurred to you. This book takes the guesswork out of how to generate, implement and evaluate your marketing strategies. How? Because a small army of experts has tested the waters on your behalf.

Over the years, each of the experts cited in this book have worked toward finding the best, most original and time-honored methods for marketing products, services and ideas. They are the people who are quoted in textbooks, featured in magazine articles, interviewed in the media and asked for advice in countless arenas. From keynoting major conferences and writing bestsellers to running their *own* businesses, these people have lived and learned the art and science of marketing. Theirs is an amalgam of expertise that touches on every aspect of how to enhance your marketing efforts creatively, efficiently and affordably.

In addition to the sheer variety and scope of the ideas presented in this book, there is also the comforting notion that marketing does not have to be difficult, complicated or laden with formal research. It can be refreshingly simple, straightforward and easy to implement. You'll find a host of ideas that cover the range from truly basic to surprisingly sophisticated. The payoff lies in the fact that every one of these ideas has been successfully used by some business owner who is blessed with no more unusual talent or skill than the average person who is struggling to make ends meet.

What this book can do for you is get you started on the road to more and better marketing efforts. Whether it's sampled in bite-sized pieces, or devoured in one fell swoop, it will stir your thinking and cause at least one "Why didn't I think of that?" every time you pick it up.

—Leann Anderson

Meet The Experts

Martin R. Baird, author of the self-published book *Guaranteed Results*, is founder of the full-service marketing management firm Robinson & Associates in Phoenix. His client roster includes the likes of Motorola, US West and Fuji North American. Baird is also a highly regarded speaker and lecturer.

Eileen Cassidy, director of international trade for the U.S. Small Business Administration, helps small businesses demystify the task of marketing their goods and services in foreign countries.

Carol Coletta, founder of Coletta & Co. in Memphis, Tennessee, is a consultant with more than 20 years of experience in community relations, public relations and corporate social responsibility. Her clients include major corporations such as Northwest Airlines, The Home Depot and Pizza Hut. Coletta has led seminars on marketing and corporate social responsibility for corporate and nonprofit clients.

Peter Connolly, formerly behind the U.S. marketing, advertising and public relations for Swedish furniture retailer Ikea, attracted the attention of American consumers and ad industry insiders alike with the store's trailblazing advertising campaign, which featured parents of adopted children, divorced parents and even gay couples. The result: an ultrahip image for Ikea and surging sales.

Rick Crandall spends his time writing, speaking and consulting on marketing and other business topics. He shows business owners, executives, managers and salespeople how to sell without being pushy by using customer-oriented marketing strategies and a consultative "soft sell." Crandall is the author of *1001 Ways to Market Your Services* and *Marketing Your Services: For People Who HATE to Sell* (both published by Contemporary/NTC). He is editor of *Marketing Magic: Proven Pathways to Success, 10 Secrets of Marketing Success: How to Jump Start Your Marketing* and *Marketing for People Not in Marketing* (all published by Select Press).

Jerry Fisher, a Los Angeles advertising copywriter, is the author and publisher of *Creating Successful Small Business Advertising* and is *Entrepreneur* magazine's "Advertising Workshop" columnist. Fisher has more than 20 years of experience in the field and has developed advertising for clients such as American Express, Mattel, Charles Schwab, Infiniti and General Mills.

Tim Girvin, principal and creative director of Tim Girvin Design Inc. in Seattle, directs the largest brand and image management consulting firm in the Pacific Northwest. He has worked on projects that span the United States and Pacific Rim, from the branding of Planet Hollywood and TV Asahi/Japan to the complete re-creation of Kraft Macaroni and Cheese packaging and brand identity. His client list includes Microsoft, Nabisco, Nordstrom, Lee Jeans, Paramount Studios and Warner Bros.

Leslie Grossman, president and founder of Communications/Marketing Action Inc. in New York City, has had a dynamic career in public relations and marketing for more than 20 years. During this time, she has created and executed programs for products and people in a broad spectrum of areas, including fashion, cosmetics, food, entertainment, business, publishing and sports. Grossman directs integrated marketing programs that include attention-getting publicity and direct-mail campaigns, in-store promotions, special events and sponsorships.

Betty Hoeffner, a senior vice president at S&S Public Relations Inc. in Northbrook, Illinois, is recognized as one of franchising's most effective marketing experts. Hoeffner has helped clients like Subway Sandwiches, Gymboree, Boston Chicken and TCBY pitch their stories to the press. Her clients have appeared on the pages of *The Wall Street Journal* and *USA Today* and have appeared on numerous TV shows, including "The Today Show" and "Good Morning America."

Bruce Judson is the author of *Net Marketing* (Wolf New Media) and a creator of Time Warner's much-praised Pathfinder Web site (www. pathfinder.com), which provides links to Time Warner's publications. Judson is regarded as one of the leading experts in the fast-emerging field of Internet marketing.

Guy Kawasaki is CEO of garage.com, a Silicon Valley-based firm that assists high-tech start-ups. Prior to this position, Kawasaki was named an Apple Fellow in 1995 in recognition of his extraordinary contribution to personal computing and his role in the acceptance of the Macintosh. He is the author of seven books, including *Rules for Revolutionaries* (HarperCollins), *The Macintosh Way* (HarperCollins), *Selling the Dream* (Harper-Collins), *How to Drive Your Competition Crazy* (Hyperion) and *Hindsights* (Warner Books).

Danielle Kennedy is the owner of sales training firm Danielle Kennedy Productions in Sun Valley, Idaho. Kennedy is also the author of six sales books—her latest is *Seven Figure Selling* (Berkley Business)—as well as audio and video sales-training programs. A sought-after speaker, she has addressed more than 1,500 corporations and professional organizations throughout the United States, Europe and Australia, and is an inductee in the Sales and Marketing Executives International Hall of Fame.

Richard Kirshenbaum and Jonathan Bond's New York City ad agency, Kirshenbaum Bond & Partners, has helped publicize clients such as Keds, Snapple, Citibank and Blimpie in the United States and abroad.

Jeanne Koester, author and publisher of *100 Tips for Starting a Small or Home-Based Business*, has run a secretarial and business support service from her Illinois home since 1992.

Jay Conrad Levinson, chairman of Guerrilla Marketing International in Mill Valley, California, has had a successful career that spans the spectrum of advertising and marketing. He is the author of *Guerrilla Marketing Weapons* (Plume), *Guerrilla Marketing, Guerrilla Selling, Guerrilla Marketing Excellence, Guerrilla Advertising* and *The Guerrilla Marketing Handbook* (all published by Houghton Mifflin). Levinson is one of the most sought-after marketing geniuses in the world. His clients have included Fortune 500 companies, national organizations, municipalities and celebrities.

Nancy Michaels is a nationally syndicated newspaper columnist, TV host, radio personality and entrepreneur who has built her reputation among clients and audiences as an authority on self-promotion and small-business marketing. Michaels is a regular contributor to business publications and is a featured speaker at business expos. She is the author of a two-cassette audio program and manual, *How to Be a Big Fish in Any Pond, Self-Marketing Strategies for Entrepreneurial Success.* Her business, Impression Impact, is located in Concord, Massachusetts.

Philip Nulman, author of *Start-Up Marketing— An Entrepreneur's Guide to Launching, Advertising, Marketing and Promoting Your Business* (Career Press), is a noted expert in the creation of campaigns for direct marketing, television, radio, sales promotion and visual merchandising. Nulman, who lives in White House, New Jersey, has written for newspapers and magazines and has appeared on radio and TV shows in every major market.

Ruth Owades, founder of San Francisco's *Calyx & Corolla*, the first-ever fresh-flower catalog, has grown her business into a $20 million-plus company sending 15 million catalogs per year to more than 1.5 million customers throughout the world.

Owades has succeeded in the highly competitive field of mail order with *Calyx & Corolla*, as well as her first venture into the field, *Gardener's Eden*, a catalog she created and sold three years later to Williams-Sonoma for $1 million. The Northern California Direct Marketing Club presented her with the 1992-93 Direct Marketer of the Year award.

Dan Peña is founder of Great Western Resources, an energy resources company in Houston. Peña started his company with a phone, a leased fax machine and less than $1,000. With these assets and a great sense for marketing, he turned the fledgling business into a $400 million corporation that he took public. Today, he leads seminars on what he calls "quantum leap methodology," the system he used to achieve much of his own success.

Diane Perlmutter is managing director of the global perception management firm Burson-Marsteller.

Al Ries is chairman of Ries & Ries, a consulting firm in Atlanta, that has done strategic work for many corporations. He is co-author of the marketing industry classic *Positioning: The Battle for Your Mind*, as well as *Marketing Warfare, Bottom-Up Marketing, Horse Sense* (all published by McGraw-Hill) and *The 22 Immutable Laws of Marketing* (HarperCollins). His latest book in the business market is *Focus:*

The Future of Your Company Depends on It (HarperBusiness).

Marlene Rossman, author of *Multicultural Marketing: Selling to a Diverse America* (Amacom), is a senior marketing and sales consultant, professor and entrepreneur. Her firm, Rossman, Graham Associates in New York City, develops sales and marketing plans for major U.S. and international companies, including AT&T, Colgate-Palmolive, Hallmark and Merrill Lynch. She coaches senior executives on domestic and international negotiating and intercultural communications and diversity/gender issues.

Michel Roux, president and CEO of Carillon Importers in Ft. Lee, New Jersey, has distinguished himself in the business community as an exceptional marketer, philanthropist, supporter of the arts and civic leader. Since 1981, he has steadfastly kept Carillon Importers at the top of the spirits industry with consistent business acumen and marketing flair. He is involved in many charitable organizations and currently sits on the boards of several companies.

Maxwell Sroge is not only one of the direct-mail industry's leading catalog consultants, but he has been responsible for starting or helping to build some of today's leading mail order businesses. Sroge has been in the mail order industry since 1959; in 1966, he founded the Maxwell Sroge Co. in Evanston, Illinois, which he has built into one of the leading catalog and direct-marketing consulting firms in the world. Clients include IBM, Phillips, RCA, Sears and a host of others.

Jack Trout, president of Greenwich, Connecticut's Trout & Partners Ltd., one of the world's most prestigious marketing firms, was instrumental in developing the marketing concept of "positioning." His firm has done work for major corporations, including AT&T, IBM, Burger King, Xerox and more. Trout is co-author of the marketing industry classic *Positioning: The Battle for Your Mind* (McGraw-Hill), as well as *Marketing Warfare* (McGraw-Hill) and *The 22 Immutable Laws of Marketing* (HarperCollins). His latest book is *The New Positioning* (McGraw-Hill).

Watts Wacker is a futurist for marketing consulting firm FirstMatter in Westport, Connecticut. He is an internationally recognized speaker and is highly sought after for spotting future consumer trends. Wacker consults on business decisions, idea generation and strategic research.

EDITH WEINER is president of Weiner, Edrich, Brown Inc. (WEB), a leading futurist consulting group in New York City. Formed in 1977, WEB has served more than 200 clients (corporate, academic and government) in identifying opportunities in the areas of marketing, product development, strategic planning, investments, human resources, public affairs and advertising. Clients have ranged from the U.S. Congress to many Fortune 500 companies. Weiner has been in the field of trend analysis and strategic planning for more than 25 years. She is acknowledged as one of the most influential practitioners of social, technological, political and economic intelligence-gathering.

Chapter 1

Plan
For Success

1

Get With The Program

From Diane Perlmutter

When it comes to successful marketing, you've got to put it in writing. Writing things down serves two purposes: It forces you to flesh out your ideas and it serves as a reminder. Write down everything you need to do to keep your customers happy. Don't forget to include a budget, a time line and a measurement system. Check your time line every week so you don't fall behind. By referring back to your marketing plan on a regular basis, you'll be able to correct small snafus before they become major problems, and you won't let any of those great marketing ideas fall by the wayside.

Money Makes The World Go Round

From Jack Trout and Al Ries

Without adequate funding, ideas won't get off the ground. Steve Jobs and Steve Wozniak had a great idea, but it was Mike Markkula's $91,000 that put Apple Computer on the map. (For his money, Markkula got one-third of Apple.) Secure sufficient financing for your venture or it won't have a chance. But start-up isn't the only period when you need financing—expansion requires a strong investment as well.

Researchers tell us that lack of adequate financing is probably the most visible reason businesses fail, and it certainly leads to problems in other areas. The costs of payroll, taxes, insurance, rent, supplies, phone service and so on add up fast. So following that time-honored rule of having one-and-a-half times as much capital as you think you'll need probably isn't such a foolish notion after all.

3

Where's Your Backup Plan?

From Michel Roux

Don't be afraid to take risks—they often bring the greatest rewards. Just make sure you always have a backup plan. In case of failure, you have to be ready to change your strategy or the formula of the product to adapt to what the market wants. You cannot look at a product and decide—bong!—it's a failure, when sometimes it's not. There may be little details in a product that are the cause of the failure, but not the concept itself. Try to find out what it is about your product that isn't working: price, packaging, name, size, quantity? A product that doesn't sell may only need a minor adjustment to be a big hit. So if your product doesn't sell well the first go-round, keep plugging away at it.

And remember, stubbornness and blind loyalty usually never pay off. Be willing to take your ego out of the equation if you want profits to add up. Call together a representative set of customers or prospects as a focus group, and get to the heart of what people really think about you, your product and your service.

ABCs Of Budgets

From Philip Nulman

If you're in the dark about how much money you should spend on marketing, don't worry. Setting a budget for your marketing efforts may be easier than you think. Every industry has a typical percentage of sales that's used for advertising and marketing. To find out your industry average, ask industry trade groups for information. Three to 5 percent of gross sales is generally a good rule of thumb for a small business.

Let's say you have an accounting business and you want more clients. Maybe the clients you have now spend an average of $500 each time they use you. And let's say they use your services at least twice a year for an average of three years. In this very simplistic example, the lifetime value of your client is $3,000. If you take only 5 percent of that amount and apply it to your marketing efforts, that would mean you would invest $150 to attract one new client. And, if your goal is to gain 10 more clients, isn't $1,500 a small price to pay for a substantial amount of new business?

The percentage you devote to marketing is just as critical to the growth of your business as the amount you budget for rent. Don't overlook its importance.

Planned Producthood

From Tim Girvin

Having a goal is the first step to achieving it. Build a pathway for how your product will be conceptualized, developed, packaged, distributed and promoted. Think about these things before you dive into production. That will help you avoid obstacles along the way and make you solve problems before they arise.

Begin by doing thorough research. Investigate the industry you're pursuing and find out from others in that industry how they are doing and what they can offer in terms of advice. Then literally put together a map showing where you are now and where you want to be. Use the "storyboard" concept that advertisers use when showing how a message will look from beginning to end. Make sure you show the major mileposts along the way that you must reach before crossing the finish line—things like developing your business plan, searching out the best location, identifying and investigating the competition, and so on.

Chapter 2

Image-Making Made Easy

Who Are You?

From Philip Nulman

Every business has something that makes it unique. Here's how to find your unique selling proposition: Examine your business and find the issues and themes that you own exclusively. Know how your business is different from its competitors and use that to your advantage. Tout your company's uniqueness in your marketing efforts.

If nothing pops out as your unique marketing feature, then take time to carefully examine what it is you offer. Revisit what made you want to get into your line of work in the first place. Ask key customers or trusted friends what they see as your distinctive characteristics. In addition, explore industry trends and look ahead to discover what you can offer first and better than anyone else.

Make A Statement

From Leslie Grossman

Create a positioning statement for your company. In one or two sentences, describe what distinguishes your business from the competition. Is it the quality of your product, the extra services you provide, the friendly staff? Whatever it is that makes your company unique, write it down. Keep it simple, memorable and snappy.

For example, if you own a floral company, what is it that sets you apart from every other florist in your area? If it's the fact that your floral arrangements are unique because of the exotic mix of flowers, foliage and artistic containers that you use, then say so in your positioning statement. For shoppers who are looking for that elegant, distinctive arrangement that will stand out in a room full of others, you will be the one they turn to if you've told them "Find a touch of the Orient in our one-of-a-kind arrangements."

Get The Look

From Leslie Grossman

I t's important to know how you are positioning your company before you start creating sales and marketing materials. Create image marketing materials that are consistent with your positioning. And whatever you do, don't scrimp. It's worth it to pay for professional logo design and marketing materials. These materials represent you, and they need to do it professionally and persuasively.

Don't make the mistake of falling into the "do it yourself with desktop publishing" mentality. Just because lots of clip art and templates exist on a software program doesn't mean they'll do when it comes to representing your company. Business cards that are proudly presented by someone who just whipped them out on her computer look second-rate. They send the message that this person (or company) must cut corners everywhere if she does it on something as relatively inexpensive as business cards.

Use It Or Lose It

From Leslie Grossman

Use your positioning statement in every written communication to customers. That's every communication—every letter, every invoice, every brochure, every flier and maybe even your business cards if your statement is only a few words long. This ensures that your message is consistent and comes across loud and clear.

A company that bakes bread from custom blends of flour reinforces its unique marketing position—"Tastes Like Home"—on the bags that contain each loaf of bread. The display racks are bordered in a running banner that also says "Tastes like home." Even the tops of the delivery trucks are painted with this phrase so that they can be seen by people looking out of skyscrapers.

10

What's Your Position?

From Leslie Grossman

Put your positioning statement to the test. On your first attempt, your statement may speak more to you and what you want from your company, but does it appeal to your target audience? Refine it until it speaks directly to their wants, needs and aspirations. If you aren't sure you're hitting the mark, ask some of your customers or potential customers what they think of it.

Better yet, call some of your customers together for a working lunch or breakfast. Ask for just a bit of their time and then get their reactions to some sample statements. Appeal to them for extreme honesty and candor, and graciously accept their remarks. Thank them and tell them you'll take their recommendations to heart as you put together your positioning statement.

Get Personal

From Dan Peña

Help define your unique selling proposition by looking at what makes you different from the owners of competing businesses. I am unique because I've become known as the $400 million man. I am the only business-success coach in the country who has built a company from scratch into $400 million, so I use that persona. Tap into what is distinctive about you (or a key employee) as an individual. If you latch on to something that strikes a chord with customers, this unique selling proposition can act as your calling card.

To come up with this nugget of information, go back over your personal history. Maybe there's something that stands out from your journey toward becoming an entrepreneur that others would relate to or admire.

12

Apart From The Rest

From Jack Trout and Al Ries

Crest fights cavities. Aim tastes good. UltraBrite whitens teeth. Close-Up freshens breath. Each brand has its own attribute. Your attribute should reflect the most appealing aspect of your business and what you think will strike a chord with customers. Choose a characteristic that sets you apart from the field and doesn't copy your competition.

Suppose you own a candy store, and most of your candies are homemade. That in itself could be your attribute. But if you're not the only store in your area that sells homemade candies, what else can you do? How about taking the lead from how the candy shops in France do their marketing? French shops package even the most humble piece or purchase in beautiful wrapping. Their presentation is exquisite, not as something extraordinary, but as a matter of course. What an extra treat it would be for buyers to have their candy purchase presented in a unique and delightful package, ready to present to a friend as a gift. Just make sure your packaging truly is distinctive and original.

13

Personality Profile

From Philip Nulman

It may sound odd, but you should create a personality for your business. Give your business human qualities that help you create a selling strategy. Define your personality by looking at your prime customers and why they buy from you. Is it because your company is fun? Reliable? Nice? Sassy? Quirky? Cutting edge? Once you know what your company's personality is, you can focus your efforts on promoting those traits.

One hardware store that prides itself on being "easy to do business with" promotes that notion in every aspect of its business. After a number of customers remarked to the owner that they "sure were easy to do business with," he took it to heart and examined all the elements he could think of regarding his ability to make customers happy. He then empowered his employees to emulate his personality and carry this philosophy forward. For you, that could mean anything from becoming a better listener to offering to make a delivery free of charge because you were going to be in the neighborhood anyway.

14

Do It Your Way

From Danielle Kennedy

Help your customers remember you by making it easy for them to associate your business with something pleasant or positive, whether it's a catchy slogan, logo, upbeat song or a free gift. Whatever it is, it can be as serious or as silly as you want. Years ago, I created my own special scratch pad with my photo on it. When I introduced myself, I handed people a free scratch pad. Soon, the whole town was making grocery lists on my face.

15

Brand News

From Tim Girvin

To sell a product successfully, you need to create brand identity that has impact. Your product is your brand. The phrase "brand new" means "fresh from the fire." Think of your brand identity as creating a lasting impression that illustrates the spirit of your product. If your product is tough and durable, or delicate and soft, you should convey that. Everything about your product—its design, name, packaging and colors—should reinforce that image.

Let's say your company prides itself in offering lightweight yet amazingly warm clothing. Your ads, illustrations, literature and demonstrations should be geared toward showing just how lightweight the clothing is. Come up with a scenario that everyone can relate to, such as a person holding clothing in one hand, and a feather in the other. While no one would believe they actually weigh the same, it creates a vivid picture that sends a clear message.

16

Fuzz Patrol

From Jack Trout

Once a brand is built, there are strong pressures to extend the equity of the brand. Be especially leery of falling prey to these pressures, or else you'll soon have an endless variety of products under the same brand. What happens? The business has made its own brand fuzzy!

The notion of doing what you do the best way you can has merit. For example, if your company has always been known as the best place to buy or rent musical instruments, then adding big screen televisions, media centers or video equipment simply doesn't fit your strengths. Don't confuse the exclusive position you might occupy by trying to be all things to all people. Become better at what you did originally.

17

Power Plays

From Jack Trout

Strong brands are always ready to beat up on their competition. And they do! But try to take business away from a great brand, and you're in for a very tough fight. You need to make sure your company is the strong brand with the upper hand.

A farm implement company in a highly productive agricultural area knew it was the region's leading supplier. The owner also knew that other implement companies in nearby communities were looking to take away a good share of his customer base. Even though he was No. 1, he knew that if he wanted to stay on top, he had to do a better job of monitoring what his competition was offering and meeting the needs of his customers. To do this, he looked at the current agricultural economy and realized his customers were struggling. Market values were down and the cost of farming was going was up. So to show how he was in touch with his customers, he opened a used implement exchange. It was a service that gave customers a place to sell their used equipment and apply the gains toward the purchase of new equipment. This attention to the real plight of his customers helped keep him in the lead.

18

Owner's Manual

From Jack Trout

Words like "overnight" are owned by brands. Domino's Pizza owns two words: "home delivery." When you think of calling for pizza, you most likely think of Domino's. You can't actually trademark a phrase like that, but if you use it enough in your sales and marketing efforts, consumers will begin to associate your company with that phrase.

In choosing such an identifying word or phrase, however, be sure that what it says about you or your company can truly be realized. If "selection, selection, selection" is what you want people to think about when they consider your company, then you had better make "selection" your number-one priority. If you think that somewhere down the line your ability to provide the "greatest selection of photo albums and frames in a 12-state region" might change, then don't use selection as your signature word. Remember, your reputation is at stake.

19

A Word Of Your Own

From Jack Trout and Al Ries

Two companies cannot own the same word in the prospect's mind. Federal Express can own "overnight," but it can't own "worldwide." DHL owns "worldwide." Don't try to usurp a word that's already associated with another company; find a word that no other company owns. That's easier than trying to muscle in on someone else's territory.

This notion applies to small businesses as well. Take a look at who your competition might be. For instance, if you operate in a regional market, then choose a distinguishing word that doesn't appear to be used by anyone else in your area. Spend some time researching and exploring possibilities. Come up with just the right word or phrase that sets you apart, and dare to be different.

Word Play

From Jack Trout and Al Ries

Once you find a word or phrase that offers a compelling glimpse of what your product or service is, use it consistently in all your written communications and marketing and advertising campaigns. Eventually, whenever that word is spoken, it will instantly make customers think of your company. Talk about free advertising.

Take, for example, the fellow who became quite an expert at sealing redwood decks and concrete driveways. He called his small company Seals on Wheels because he would make house calls, office calls or stops at any location that called for his services. And, as you would suspect, he used the image of a slippery little seal as part of his logo. Since the word "seal" can be used in a variety of ways (seal the deal, seal it shut, etc.), his business name and logo were reinforced even when the situation didn't necessarily have anything to do with his business.

The Name Game

From Tim Girvin

A carefully considered product name is key to consumer recognition and recall. Poorly named products often fail because there is no memory connection. Great names build imagery in the minds of consumers. Good names are also easy to pronounce. Customers are less likely to ask for a product by name if they can't figure out how the heck to say it. Great names also grow with a company.

In fact, before you start thinking up names for your new business, try to define the qualities to be identified with your business. If you're starting a hearth-baked bread shop, for example, you might want a name that conveys freshness, warmth and a homespun atmosphere. Immediately, you can see that names like "Kathy's Bread Shop" or "Arlington Breads" would communicate none of these qualities. But consider the name "Open Hearth Breads." The bread sounds homemade, hot and just out of the oven. And later, as you diversify a bit, you could become "Open Hearth Bakery," enabling you to hold on to your suggestive name without totally mystifying your established clientele.

Do Some Soul Searching

From Tim Girvin

Once you name your product, you need to inject it with soul. Every product needs a heart or core spirit to build on. Take the time to initiate a core value you can build on as you develop your product. Focusing on the values you started with, present a coherent vision of your product through color, product design, packaging and more.

Tools that are built to last a lifetime need to look the part as well as perform flawlessly. The soul of a quality tool company rests with its commitment to building something that lasts. After all, what good does it do to have a tool that lasts forever if it doesn't quite do the job when you use it? From the first second a prospect lays eyes on the tool, to the moment its packaging is torn away, to the first time he or she holds it, the message has to be quality, sturdiness, precision.

23

Package Perfect

From Tim Girvin

Packaging is a message platform to channel your ideas to the consumer . . . fast! Package your product creatively for a big impact. Make your package bold, a "fast storyteller" and reflective of your product's personality. Take a good, hard look at what you're selling. What colors, textures or images come to mind? The packaging should give consumers an idea of what your product is just by its shape and colors. You want a real attention-grabber so that a consumer walking down the aisle of a store would immediately be drawn to your products.

And what about your competitors? Does a particular shape come to mind every time you think of their products?

As with your logo, graphics and communications pieces, packaging often calls for the hand of a professional designer. Put together a few samples for a comparison session with potential customers. Feedback is essential to have before manufacturing ever starts. And, if you already have a product on the shelves, do some ongoing research to see if the packaging is doing its job.

24

The Color Of Money

From Tim Girvin

When it comes to creating a strong brand identity, choose an array of colors for your product and packaging that you can "own." Palettes that are too generic diminish your product's presence. Aim to dominate your shelf position with color. Whatever colors the competition is using, use a different mix to make your product stand out. Once you find colors you like, stick with them to build brand recognition. Your goal? Make that color so recognizable that when consumers see it, they automatically think of your product.

One produce company took an unusual approach to marketing by choosing a vegetable that reflects a distinct and different color combination. Instead of the trusty tomato or leafy green lettuce, the company chose an eggplant and presented it in a brilliant, deep aubergine and vivid olive green. All this was set against a bright white stock. It looked smashing and captured customers' attention every time they saw that combination.

25

Stand And Deliver

From Tim Girvin

Designing your product is all-important, but don't forget to pay attention to merchandising. If your product will be sold on sales racks or distribution stands, make sure those displays combine design elements that will complement your products. In addition to the design factor, your equipment has to be functional. Create a structure that works with your product's size and shape, and make sure it's easy for your distribution channels to use. Test it with them to confirm that they are comfortable with your strategy.

For instance, suppose you have a line of costume jewelry that is colorful and lightweight. It will need to be displayed in a way that allows the customer to see as many pieces as possible. But if you know there will be limited space available in boutiques, you'll want to design a display case that doesn't take up much counter space and won't be easily tipped over. Have several people "browse" your display ahead of time so that you can get their feedback. Ask questions like: Was it easy to see my pieces? Could you select and return pieces to their places easily? Did my display catch your eye?

26

Get The Big Picture

From Tim Girvin

If your products revolve around an entire concept, think of ways to create brand presence from the start. From the moment consumers see your shop, your uniforms or your vehicles, memory connections are built. Consumers have great memories if the imagery you provide is consistent. Recurring design elements or colors can create instant recognition, so repeat your logo, signature color or other design element throughout your store—on the walls, on your sign, on your vehicles.

Let's say a bicycle shop has incorporated into its logo the spokes of a wheel. The name of the shop might also have the letter "o" somewhere in the name. If that's the case, then every time the letter "o" is used in the logo, it should look like the spokes of a wheel. Just think how often that image could appear in the name "Cook's Bicycle Shop." Price tags, water bottles, fanny packs, work shirts and more could sport the unique wheel logo in colors that reinforce the shopper's memory.

Office Attire

From Leslie Grossman

Ask yourself a question: Does your office communicate the image you're selling? If customers visit your place of business, make sure it sells who you are. That doesn't mean big expenditures; it means using creativity and ingenuity. If your company is in the high-tech industry, sleek black and chrome will make your office look the part. If you sell antique jewelry, a few pieces of antique furniture will set the mood.

But regardless of what the overall decor might be, it needs to be appropriate for your business and nicely put together. That means things should be arranged in a way that welcomes your customers and makes them feel like they understand the place. Too much clutter, too many design elements and too many choices can be confusing and upsetting to a customer. Walking into an office and not knowing where to go is not only thoughtless, it's bad business. Seeing clutter, dead plants or barren or overloaded walls sends a message that the business doesn't care and doesn't attend to detail. Your look should inspire confidence in your clients and customers.

Chapter 3

Get Cozy
With Your
Customers

Men Are From Mars, Women Are From Venus

From Watts Wacker

Men and women are exploring what heretofore was the domain of the opposite sex. Men are becoming more introspective, while women are becoming more hedonistic. This notion has given rise to the term "SNAG" (sensitive, new-age guys)—guys who are part machismo and part wimp. It's something men have been longing to try—and they're finally getting their chance. Marketers can tap into men's new-found sensitivity with products and services that appeal to their "feminine side." For instance, more and more men are realizing the joy of cooking. A wise marketer is the one whose direct-mail pieces promoting a revolutionary line of cookware go to men and women alike.

By the same token, women are becoming more active, and they're participating in and watching more sports— just look at the number of new magazines geared to women and fitness. That indicates there will be a rise in the number of products and services designed specifically for the active woman.

Crossing Over

From Edith Weiner

Trend spotters tell us that all products and services are becoming crossovers; you can no longer assume a difference between, for instance, a residential and a commercial customer. What's right for one may also be right for the other. Indeed, so many customers are entrepreneurs themselves that work and home are melding. Likewise, don't assume traditional distinctions between urban, suburban and rural residents. City people are moving out to the hinterlands because they can be technologically connected anywhere; rural dwellers are moving into cities in search of opportunity. Don't make assumptions about customers—they could backfire.

For instance, deciding not to send a direct-mail piece promoting a sophisticated camera and security system to someone whose address is Rural Route 6, Outback, Nevada, could be a big mistake. Today, many people choose to operate their businesses from locations that are off the beaten path. But that doesn't mean they don't need ample security to protect their investment.

Get Personal

From Ruth Owades

Have a clear idea of your customer. Marketing can be focused only if you really understand the psychographics and demographics of your customer. Find out as much as you can about your target market—age ranges, gender, socioeconomic standing, regions, buying habits and more. You can never know too much about your customers.

For example, if you own a lawn and garden business, and if your ideal-customer profile tells you that your most profitable customers own their homes and like to work in the yard, then there is little point in making a personal pitch to people who live in condos or apartments. Go after the people who fit your profile with a personal message and an offer for a free tool or bottle of plant food.

31

Down With The Masses

From Watts Wacker

L ook at the individuality in America. We tend to view the 260 million people living in the United States as a mass market. But there are no mass answers anymore. If you take 100 people who have one foot on a block of ice and the other foot in a fireplace, you can argue that the average person is comfortable. In reality, no one's average. And that goes for all the various segments of our population, too. Whether you're talking about ethnic, gender, socioeconomic or regional groups, you have to remember that everyone within those groups is an individual. You've got to stop looking for mass solutions.

One way to do this is to develop a strong database. With the help of technology, it's easy to set up a file on every customer you have, with numerous fields that indicate what makes each customer unique. After all, the more information you have about your customers, the more powerful your ability to reach them in a customized, personal way. Today's consumer is looking for an island of personalization in a sea of one-size-fits-all.

32

Like Old, Like New

From Al Ries

If you want to know what your new customers will be like, take a good long look at your existing customers. New customers most likely will be similar to old customers. The more you know about the people you do business with now, the easier it will be to find new people to do business with. To find out more about your customers, make it a habit to have them fill out a short survey when they make a purchase, and ask questions relevant to your business.

For instance, if you sell sporting equipment, ask your customer questions like: What sports do you participate in? Do you have family members who play sports? If you have children, what are their ages and what sports do they like? Are you at the beginner, intermediate or advanced level? What equipment are you looking at for your next purchase? What part of the city do you live in? This kind of information allows you to put together a profile of who your best customers are and who you should look to as potential customers.

Be Your Own Customer

From Martin R. Baird

Want to know what your customers are really after? How about spending a couple of days in their shoes. What activities do they squeeze into their day? What kinds of services and products do they want? At what time of day is it convenient for them to visit a business like yours? To find out what your customers really want, visit a wide range of businesses they're likely to frequent. Observe how customers are treated, as well as the kinds of services that appear important to them; then adapt your business accordingly.

If you happen to have a custodial or cleaning service, what better way to judge what's important to your clients than to see how they work and what they expect from others? If you notice that they receive frequent deliveries and have little time to properly handle or store the items when they arrive, why not suggest a "holding bin" be set aside, and your crew will handle putting any leftover items away when they come in to clean? Cleaning and picking up could be a service that would make a big difference to that client. But there's no way of knowing that until you walk a mile in their shoes.

34

Getting To Know You

From Jay Conrad Levinson

The key to short- and long-term profitability is to be involved with your customers, as demonstrated by your follow-up, and for them to be involved with you, as demonstrated by their repeat business. To get involved with your customers, you've got to get to know them. Talk to them when they visit your store, ask their opinions on merchandise, solicit recommendations for items they'd like to see, and find out how they use your products. The same goes for service businesses—the more you know about your customers, the more you can interact with them in meaningful ways.

One company that specializes in camera and video repair asks customers if it can take a quick photo of them to put with their files. This little gesture not only provides for a good laugh from time to time, but becomes a shared experience and a conversation point each time the customer returns. It can act as a bridge to other topics and allows the owner of the company to get to know his customers in a personal way.

Do Your Homework

From Eileen Cassidy

Before you jump the gun and start designing a marketing campaign, you need to make sure you have all the information you need. Research is key to creating a marketing strategy that works. And it doesn't have to cost a bundle. Take advantage of the U.S. government's free information sources before taking the plunge. Start with the Small Business Administration's Web site (www.sba.gov) and the Office of International Trade's Web page (www.sba.gov/oit).

In addition, you may want to contact the professional or trade associations that represent the industry you're part of. If you happen to be in the landscaping or lawn maintenance business, investigate what your industry says is the hot trend of the day. Maybe you'll learn that in your area xeriscaping is becoming quite popular. Or perhaps data will show that anticipated growth for new homes is heading your way. That information could give you a leg up on competition, especially if you market the fact that you "take the headache out of putting in a new lawn."

36

What Price Research?

From Jerry Fisher

Did you know that you can do market research yourself by sending questionnaires to customers? Try sending an unexpected $2 bill along with a questionnaire asking customers about their product or service preferences. Make sure you ask no more than six questions and word them so that they are easy to understand but specific to your business. The response you get to just a few simple questions could be like mining gold—you have to dig a little bit, but the $2 bill helps to loosen the soil. It also lets them know you want to please them, and gives a delightful incentive to fill out the questionnaire. You'd be surprised how much greater your response rate will be by simply slipping in a little cash. At $2 per customer, that's some cheap market research.

37

Changing Places

From Leann Anderson

Warning! Marketers—be ready for change. People's lives are changing constantly; they are marrying, divorcing, remarrying; changing jobs and careers; feeling secure one day and insecure the next. Don't assume you can pigeonhole your customers because of what they buy or tell you now. Be ready to accept the fact that a customer may buy sexy lingerie today and combat boots tomorrow, or may want a piece of electronic equipment with all the bells and whistles this week but something basic the next week.

That's why it's so important to take your customers' "buying temperature" regularly. Make it easy for them to give you feedback. A special 800 number for customer comments, an e-mail address that's easy to remember or access, a suggestion box with cards and pencils prominently displayed—all these methods allow for feedback you should want and need. Remember, however, that none of this information is worth a floppy disk if it doesn't get recorded somewhere in your customer database.

38

Play By The Numbers

From Marlene Rossman

Ask any marketing analyst and he or she will vouch for the value of good research. The great thing is, it's easy to get Census Bureau data for the communities where you plan to sell your products and services. Key to this process, however, is knowing what to look for. Before you tap these sources, know what types of people or businesses would be drawn to your product or service. Have a clear notion of who your ideal customer might be. Develop a profile with as many traits or characteristics as you can reasonably put together so that when you do your research, you know what to spot.

The numbers are free, and one look will tell you if the community has the groups you should be targeting. And now, thanks to the Web, it's even easier to get your hands on Census Bureau statistics. Just point your browser to www.census.gov.

Chapter 4

Go Crazy
With
Creativity

39

Think Small

From Edith Weiner

Don't be afraid to focus on the smaller market because for every trend there's at least one countertrend. It's actually better sometimes to focus on a smaller market— one nobody is serving because they're all off catering to the bigger trend. You could corner the market in the smaller arena and have more customers and higher sales than if you try to snag a share of the bigger market. And if the trend shifts (as they always do), you could end up as the top brand in a fast-growing market.

Consider this: One small business that specialized in repairing household appliances found it had quite a corner on a smaller market. It advertised itself as the "dinosaur specialist" because it was one of the few companies that could repair appliances that were old or no longer being produced. It found there were an awful lot of people who hated to part with things like their favorite toaster, even though they could afford new ones. This specialty developed quite by accident, but the owner was wise enough to know he was filling a niche that no one else seemed to want.

Goodbye, Rules

From Guy Kawasaki

Change the rules of the game. If the odds are stacked against you, don't play by the established rules. Change distribution, pricing, support or marketing—somehow create your own advantages. If all your competitors are headed in one direction, take a different tack and you'll have a better chance of making a name for yourself.

Say, for example, you own a dry cleaning business and you've noticed your competition is big on drive-thru service. Maybe your next move should be to de-emphasize your drive-thru window and focus on promoting your free delivery service. Investigate the relative costs involved ahead of time so that what you offer really is affordable. But chances are the extra business you generate will more than cover your costs.

41

Be No. 1

From Jack Trout

The *first* in almost every category tends to become the well-known brand. While the business world buzzes about quality, the real success stories are the ones that are first. Instead of following the crowd and opening the 10th coffeehouse in town, do something no one else has done before.

Just think about the bagel business. For years the breakfast pastry of choice was probably the doughnut. From coast to coast, it was the snack the masses ate with their morning coffee. What a revolution when the first bagel shop appeared on the same block as the doughnut factory! Now bagels are practically a ritual for many people. The key to the bagel shop success came with being the *first* one in the neighborhood. After all, that's how Starbucks, Domino's and even McDonald's got their start.

Rock On

From Philip Nulman

When it comes to marketing, you should live by the R.O.C.K. (Roundtable of Competitive Knockouts) rule. Once a month sit down—either by yourself or with others—and develop at least a dozen knockout marketing ideas. Don't limit yourself in any way in these brainstorming sessions—don't be afraid to think big or small. Come up with ideas you can implement immediately, as well as ideas for the future. Consider what your competition is doing and how you can keep them off-balance, and you'll be perceived as the most innovative marketer in your area.

Let's say you own a bookstore. Your goal for the coming month might be to develop 12 marketing ideas geared toward selling more of your children's books. Pull out all the stops and start generating ideas about *where* to place your marketing efforts and *how* to make them appeal to kids, parents and grandparents. You might even want to target only 3- to 7-year-olds. Preschools, day-care facilities and playgrounds immediately come to mind. Now, go for it.

43

Button Up

From Martin R. Baird

Did you know you can draw attention to yourself in a very simple way? Try wearing a button every day. Sporting an intriguing button on your lapel is a sure-fire conversation starter that can lead to, well, who knows what? Use every conversation as an opportunity to talk about your business and what you do. Have five or six buttons made up with silly, funny or insightful sayings, and wear them to public events, speaking engagements and business meetings.

Try wearing a button that says "I love chocolate" and offering a Hershey's Kiss to the people you greet. Or how about a button that says "Save the Squingles." Since nobody knows what a "squingle" is, you'll get lots of questions and more than a few smiles. Just be sure to have an answer ready when they ask. Rest assured, this tactic will also ensure that people won't forget you, and in business, being memorable can make the difference between a customer calling your company or calling the competition.

Creative Differences

From Watts Wacker

Creativity is becoming a much bigger motivating issue than ever before. Creativity has gone from being something that's nice to have in your life to a necessity— not only in the business world but in people's personal lives. Some people are already exploring their artistic side with hobbies in the areas of visual arts and music. But it's a need we haven't fulfilled because of time pressures. So creativity becomes a megatrend for the future, especially as baby boomers get closer to retirement age, which means they'll finally have more time on their hands to partake in creative activities.

Consider the recent craze for creating thematic, decorative scrapbooks and photo albums. When the great minds behind this idea started marketing it, they realized that people who have time on their hands, guilt in their hearts and box after box of unlabeled, unsorted photographs would flock to classes where they could acquire albums, tools and stickers to make creating a beautiful (or even just functional) scrapbook a pleasurable and productive pastime. It took real creativity to market a solution to a universal problem in a way that was fun and profitable.

Fax Attack

From Martin R. Baird

Don't waste any opportunity to entice customers to buy from you. Turn even the most mundane communications with customers into sales opportunities. For instance, try this success secret: Make the most of your fax cover sheets. In addition to the usual information—name, address, phone and fax numbers, e-mail address—use the cover to promote the specials and savings you're offering, or as a means of simply saying "Thanks." One florist even uses his fax sheet to continually remind people of the next big holiday on the horizon. Whatever you choose to say, make sure you revise it at least every three months or so. Since you're already sending a fax, it's like a free ad.

Serve It Up

From Rick Crandall

Customers often have trouble plunking down their cold hard cash for intangible services. They're much more comfortable if they can walk away with a purchase they can touch and feel. You can make what you do more palpable by offering a package deal that gives your service some semblance of a product.

For example, a massage therapist may want to offer a discount card when customers buy 10 massages. The therapist punches the card for each massage. Or consider providing legal advice for a year at a set fee. This may be more desirable to customers who are scared away by the prospect of open-ended billing.

Share And Share Alike

From Guy Kawasaki

Seize segments, not shares. Market share alone doesn't result in profitability. The way to become profitable is to seize and satisfy niches. Then you might gain market share, too.

While some dealers sell all types of boats and marine vehicles, a wise business owner in the Northwest decided he wouldn't even try to compete with the big guys who sell thousands of boats each month. Instead, he went for deep penetration in the fishing boat market. And not just any kind of fishing boat. He offered the high-end, custom variety. His niche was small, but very loyal and lucrative.

48

Go Against The Flow

From Nancy Michaels

A great idea for anyone responsible for marketing a business is to offer promotions at unusual times. Instead of offering special deals at Christmas like every other business on the face of the planet, why not commemorate a less celebrated holiday? On St. Patrick's Day, offer specials on anything you sell that's green. Or on Cinco de Mayo, offer a 5 percent discount on everything in the store. To add a more personal touch, remember your clients' birthdays. By going against the grain, you'll draw attention to your business and lure customers during traditionally slow periods.

49

Card Sharks

From Martin R. Baird

Traditional business cards don't do the job when it comes to marketing. If all your card does is give out your company's address and phone number, it isn't working hard enough for you. Smart marketers know that business cards can do much more. Why not try using both sides of business cards? Use the back of your cards to let people know about extra services you provide that they may not be aware of. On the front, display your phone number prominently and include a few words emphasizing the benefits of your business.

Or consider making your business card a reflection of your personality. Without getting too cutesy, have one of your favorite quotes printed on the back. Suppose you happen to own a store specializing in gourmet cookware or ingredients. Turning a card over and reading "A good cook is like a sorceress who dispenses happiness. —*Elsa Schiaparelli*" is a treat in itself.

You May Be A Winner

From Jerry Fisher

ather more prospects—creatively. You can count on contests to pull prospects in and get them involved with your business in a nonsales environment. Sponsoring a contest also promotes your company as a fun, friendly firm, which makes you and your business more appealing.

For instance, a dating service may run a contest called "Who Loves Who?" in newspaper ads. The ads show the smiling faces of six male former members on one side of the ad and on the other side, the six women they met through the service. The object is to match the women to the men they met and married through the dating service. The winner receives a free membership. More important, however, is that all the people who enter the contest are considered prime prospects for the service and receive a telemarketing pitch to join.

51

Divide And Conquer

From Jack Trout and Al Ries

Over time, a category will divide and become two or more categories. Computers used to be a single category, but now there are computers, mainframes, minicomputers, fault-tolerant computers, supercomputers, workstations and PCs. But, if you can't develop an entirely new category for what you want to offer, try to create a category within an existing category. That way, you'll be seen as a leader.

One businesswoman saw this as an opportunity to set herself apart from her competition. She ran a dog-grooming service and was literally getting clipped by the other businesses that could handle more and larger animals than she could. So instead of bowing out, she became the czar of care for small, exotic dog breeds. She developed a category within a category and trained her staff to see themselves as grooming specialists, too.

52

Dare To Be Different

From Peter Connolly

t may sound frightening, but you have to take chances and risks. If you don't try, you'll never know. The only way to succeed in today's fierce marketplace is by daring to be different (but only with good reason). If you don't have a compelling reason to do something out of the ordinary, being different can backfire on you. In general, however, consumers appreciate companies that show individuality, commitment and passion. The more initiative you take, the more you will be looked at as an innovator. There can only be one leader, and that can only result from taking some chances.

That's exactly what the owners of Three Dog Bakery did when they started their unusual enterprise. What started out as a joke (Mom tucking a bone-shaped cookie cutter into a Christmas stocking) became a lucrative business when the owners moved from making a batch of dog cookies to barrels of them. They are now proud bakers of pupcakes, Scottie biscotti, Great Danish and collie-flowers. All sell like hotcakes, and customers love the company. Daring to be different took them from a $1,000 investment to $10 million in sales.

53

Go The Distance

From Leann Anderson

Sometimes the age-old saying "You can lead a horse to water . . ." has to be ignored. Why? Because success can come from simply taking your product or service directly to the customer. Sometimes seeing, trying, tasting, whatever, is believing. If you have a product or service that simply has to be experienced to be appreciated, then that's exactly what you'll have to do—deliver the experience.

One couple who started a company called Buddies Better Bagels knew they had to get people to sample their goods to generate business. So they started dropping in on local businesses and leaving free samples of their baked goods. From giant factories to small offices, they used a creative "buddy system" to get the word out. They developed a costume for a pair of their employees to wear that made them look like they were attached at the hip. They hired eight college students to act as their four sets of "buddies" and deliver their products to various companies. Not only did the people at the workplace appreciate a tasty treat, but they got a good laugh from the "three-legged" pair as they walked through the office.

Tune In, Not Out

From Michel Roux

Be attuned to the world around you. Inspiration is everywhere. It's important to listen to people's ideas, and that means everybody's ideas. Don't count anybody out. Everyone can come up with a stellar idea—your secretary, your lawyer, your accountant, your spouse. They may help you see things you've missed or see something in a new light. And always encourage everyone around you to spout off their ideas, whether they are directly related to your business or not—sometimes a nonrelated idea can plant the seed for another idea that's even better.

A fellow who owns a vending company was patiently waiting for a haircut. Another man was talking to one of the staff and mentioned that he sure wished he could get an antacid or an aspirin from the same vending machine where he buys his coffee. Well, to make a long story short, the vending company now has a variety of supplemental items like aspirin and antacid in some of its machines. Who would have guessed?

55

Go Against The Grain

From Dan Peña

Another tip for savvy marketers lies in doing things that are 180 degrees against conventional wisdom. For example, about 100 years ago, the British were trying to scale the Matterhorn. For almost 70 years, many men and women died in the effort. Then one day, a gentleman decided to take a different route: Rather than go up the south slope, he went up the north slope. From that angle, you could stroll right up to the top. In the face of 100 years of conventional wisdom, he decided to do exactly the opposite. Many times, that's just what it takes.

Consider General Motors' Saturn experience: It decided to build a car that had one price, a lifetime guarantee, and no extras, sales commission or pressure. It was completely against the conventional wisdom—but it worked.

56

Bad News Is Good News

From Jack Trout and Al Ries

Don't be afraid to sell a negative. Just consider the following example: Listerine admitted that its product tasted bad ("The taste you hate twice a day"), but customers interpreted that to mean it killed a lot of germs. If you can find something about your business that you can joke about but that conveys a strong message, go with it.

For instance, one tropical-produce vendor took pride in the wide variety of uses he found for coconuts. But people who shopped at his market walked right past his coconut bin. He decided to capitalize on the hairy, little product by creatively displaying the coconuts under a colorful sign that read "The ugly fruit with the beautiful taste!" Sales went up.

Selling The Sizzle

From Dan Peña

Marketing in the '90s is about selling intangibles. To sell concepts, things and ideas, you need to be able to break away from the pack. Everybody in the marketing business knows how to write headlines that grab the reader. What they may not know is that now they have to create different headlines using different marketing strategies. What you need to do is change your mind-set so your marketing and advertising campaigns convey the intangible, not the tangible, advantages of your product or service.

Suppose you own an ice cream parlor. Today's health-conscious consumer may need to be drawn to your product in a new way. Why not market the memory of the days when taking time out for a chocolate soda or an ice cream sundae was a pleasure beyond compare? Sell the quiet, peaceful good ol' days along with that Jamocha Almond Fudge.

Get Out Of That Rut

From Peter Connolly

Consumers are exposed to so many options that it is critical to find ways to break through the clutter. How? By seeking new channels that complement the brand and your customers' profiles. This applies to all aspects of marketing: finding alternative advertising media, keying in on new ways to reach your market, and zeroing in on innovative distribution methods. Get creative in all areas of your marketing and don't feel like you have to follow some proven formula.

A car wash company that also does detailing for all sorts of vehicles takes great pleasure in sending its correspondence in off-white envelopes speckled with textured brown ink. Across the corner is printed "Time for a wash?" Talk about unconventional marketing. Who could ignore that creative envelope?

Anything Goes

From Watts Wacker

Consider the "Slinky cyclicity" theory of history—history is a pendulum that goes back and forth. But history does more than that. It also continually tumbles forward, like a Slinky set in motion. That means there are times when consumers go for consensus, and times when they want to explore contrasting points. Right now people are exploring contrasts. What that means for marketers is that people will unexpectedly try new things—and you will have great success selling products as diverse as Ben & Jerry's ice cream and nonfat frozen yogurt. What that means for business owners is that you don't necessarily have to follow major trends. You can introduce a product that's 180 degrees opposite of what the bestseller in your category is and still find a niche.

Consider, for instance, one company that manufactures high-end teak furniture. Its owners pride themselves in producing the best of the best; nothing inexpensive finds its way into their inventory. But when they realized they had lots of leftover teak that wasn't being used, they developed an inexpensive line of toothpicks and back scratchers that helped put the leftover bits and pieces to good use.

Chapter 5

Try The
Buddy System

Howdy, Partner

From Diane Perlmutter

Want to increase the scope of your marketing efforts without spending any additional dollars? It may sound too good to be true, but you can do just that by partnering with other companies that sell complementary yet noncompetitive products and services to your target market. In this way, you get twice the exposure at half the cost.

For instance, if you run a Web design firm, you might want to link up with a local Internet service provider that can pass leads on to you. Or if you sell nutritional supplements, you might want to join forces with a local gym where you could give seminars about nutrition to health-conscious members.

Get A Piggyback Ride

From Dan Peña

Market on the backs of other well-known names. Develop a joint venture with Wal-Mart or Nordstrom to market a product. With this kind of arrangement, you get to take advantage of their well-known names and their powerful marketing machines. You may have to pony up some money, but what you get in return can be very worthwhile—increased exposure, your product linked with a highly visible, well-respected entity, and strong distribution channels. People won't ask you whether it's a 90-10 deal; they'll assume it's 50-50. So by definition, you're uplifted one, two or even three levels. Let's say you own a small company that makes unique, gourmet food items. This piggyback tactic could be especially effective for you because large department stores love to carry exclusive items that make great gifts or stocking stuffers during the holidays.

And don't think you have to go with a large, national firm. If your marketplace is regional instead of national, you might find it just as rewarding to distribute your product or promote your service through a compatible company that's also regional.

Seminar Smarts

From Rick Crandall

Here's a tip worth talking about: Consider the benefits of getting together with other entrepreneurs whose services complement yours and marketing a series of seminars. By teaming with other business owners, you'll increase the number of possible attendees. A bonus to the group method: If you're not used to giving speeches, sharing the stage could calm your nerves. If you've got a terrible case of stage fright, you can also host a panel about a certain topic. Even though you aren't one of the main speakers, you still come off as the expert since you're the one hosting the event.

Health-care companies do this all the time. A seminar on the importance of exercise in your life could feature a panel made up of a physician or exercise physiologist, a conditioning spa owner, a dietician, the owner of a sporting goods store, someone affiliated with a shoe company, or even a cosmetics consultant.

Promo Partners

From Tim Girvin

Look for promotional alliances or partners for your product. This doesn't necessarily mean that money has to change hands, but sometimes joint promotions are an easy way to piggyback products. These promotions can be a real bonus to your business, providing additional exposure to consumers of the partner product, not to mention reduced promotional costs since you're sharing expenses with your partner. Plus, the partner you choose doesn't have to have an obvious connection to your product or service.

Here's an illustration of how a couple of completely unrelated companies located near one another pulled off a joint promotion. A greenhouse that handles both perennials and annuals and a combination coffee shop and bakery thought it would be great to sponsor a "Stop and Smell the Roses" promotion, during which anyone who made a purchase at either place received a coupon for 20 percent off another purchase at the partner's business. The promotion only lasted for one week, but it brought in lots of new customers for both partners.

Mentor Mania

From Dan Peña

Find people who have marketed more successfully than you have, and seek their assistance. You'll find these people are very open to sharing their ideas. Make a list of the people you admire in your industry and in other industries as well. Other fields often use marketing techniques that could work in any arena, so don't count people out just because they're in the manufacturing business and you provide a service. Be sure to use the information they give you. Create a plan of action based on what you've learned. Follow up with mentors to inform them of your successes and how their advice made it possible. And always, always thank your mentors for their valuable time and insight.

Co-Dependency's OK

From Jay Conrad Levinson

Stop worrying about your competition and start thinking of ways to cooperate with other businesses through marketing tie-ins, known as fusion marketing. You're dependent on other businesses, your customers, employees and even your suppliers. Take advantage of their contacts and their customer lists by forging some joint marketing projects. If you help them and they help you, everyone thrives.

Suppose you own a graphics design firm. Wouldn't it make sense for you to team up with a nearby printer and a public relations firm to share leads and make referrals? Often, businesses need brochures designed but have no idea where to have them printed. You could easily suggest the printing company you've "partnered" with. And it's always a good idea for a company wise enough to have a professional design group do its brochure to also investigate the benefits of generating some good PR. With this arrangement, several reputable businesses can support and promote each other.

Kid Stuff

From Jerry Fisher

Many companies have found that if they package a widget that appeals to children along with their products, the parents will follow. Fast-food franchises learned this trick a long time ago. Their smartest marketing ploy, next to "extra value" meal combinations, has been the invention of the "kid's fun pack" meal. Each month, an inexpensive new plastic widget is bundled with a child-sized burger-and-fries combination to draw kids and (drag) parents in for a meal. If you're the parent of a 4- to 7-year-old, you know it works. To get in on the action without shelling out a lot of cash for widgets, partner with a children's business or toy manufacturer that can provide you with goodies.

Channel Surfing

From Edith Weiner

Realize that no delivery channel is sacred anymore. Your competitors are bypassing existing channels, and if you stay chained to the traditional way of doing business, you're missing out on several opportunities to expand your sales. You should be searching for as many strategic marketing alliances as possible so you can diversify your ability to meet customer demand and face competitive pressures. By teaming up with other business owners, you maximize your ability to reach customers and meet their needs.

So why not try analyzing the types of customers you have? What types of businesses are they in? What other companies do they do business with? If you spot a significant number of your customers coming from one industry or one neighborhood, consider teaming up with other suppliers or vendors that also might supply your customers. Look into the future and do some scouting for unlikely but timely partners.

Chapter 6

Put Your
Customers
To Work

Keep In Touch

From Diane Perlmutter

Getting customers to buy from you once will boost your business, but what will really boost your bottom line is getting them to buy from you again and again. You need to develop a follow-up system to stay in regular contact with customers so they'll think of you when they're ready to buy again. It doesn't have to be expensive or time-consuming. Simply mail a postcard or send an e-mail message to remind customers that it's time to reorder, or better yet, create an automatic reordering system so your product is sent directly and customers are billed automatically.

The key to making this work is technology. If you want your business to grow through keeping in touch with customers, it is vital to have a system that doesn't take up an unreasonable amount of time. With the right program, you'll be able to flag important information, set up fields specific to your business, and with the touch of a key, print out the names of customers who will receive your special attention.

Watch your industry magazines for advertised software, talk with others about what they use, or have a computer consultant set up your magic communications system.

Don't Leave Me

From Edith Weiner

Keeping customers is far more lucrative than finding new ones. Focus on your relationships with existing buyers and find ways to hang on to them. And if they leave, do as much research to find out why as you do to seek out new markets. But getting this information is only half the battle; you have to do something with it. If past customers say your store wasn't open early enough in the morning, then change your hours. If the service wasn't friendly enough, give your employees some customer service training.

Whatever the reason for leaving might be, have a plan in place for taking action. When the owner of a vacuum cleaner business noticed his clientele was slipping away, he went through his records to see how many repeat customers he had and also developed a list of the one-time buyers. Then he had one employee, plus himself, call all the people who had stopped doing business with him. They had a script written, some key questions prepared, forms to fill out, and a "thank you" coupon ready to mail to each person they called. Plus, they specifically asked if they could have a second chance.

Happy Birthday!

From Jerry Fisher

A good piece of advice for any marketer is to record the birth dates of all your customers so that on that day, or the week before, they'll get a special greeting from you. You may want to offer a special birthday discount—$10 off any purchase or 15 percent off all purchases that day. Sentimentality earns you brownie points—and that translates into sales!

Let's say you own a company that sells figurines. If you start a birthday club, you can offer the person celebrating the birthday a free figurine with the purchase of another one on that day. Send the honoree a coupon in advance and encourage the recipient to share it with friends and family. That way, customers who want twice the bang for their buck might seek you out when buying a gift for the birthday honoree.

The Customer Is King

From Diane Perlmutter

Don't take existing customers for granted, or your existing customers may become someone else's new customers. If you don't treat them well, you can bet someone else will. Think of your current customers as if they were still unsold potential buyers. They deserve just as much attention as new customers. Simple things like returning their phone calls and staying in contact after a sale will improve your chances of keeping your customers from deserting you.

An example of treating your current customer royally can be found with one company that does tree and shrub trimming. It not only reminds each customer early in the spring to schedule trimming before the crunch starts, but it also leaves a small potted seedling for each customer to either plant in his or her own yard or share with someone in the community that might need help with landscaping.

72

Pay Up!

From Al Ries

Tell customers you will pay a finder's fee for each new customer they send you. The fee doesn't have to be expensive—and it doesn't have to be a cash payment. You can offer one of your products for free or offer a free service. America Online has become the biggest online service in part by rewarding members with a free month of service for every customer they refer.

The key here is to be creative, generous and reliable. Whatever you decide to offer as an incentive for referrals, make sure it has value to the customer. Business owners often miss the mark on this effort by offering something that is of little value to them and, consequently, of lesser value to the customer. Don't use this as an opportunity to unload stagnant inventory. If a customer thinks enough of you to refer someone to you, show your appreciation promptly and generously.

Customer Comeback

From Jerry Fisher

Getting those customers who have strayed back in the fold takes creative measures. Here's another way to bring lost customers back to your business: reactivation vouchers. Mail a $20 no-strings-attached voucher to any customers you haven't seen in six months or longer. Few can turn it down, and still fewer will spend only $20.

This effort can be especially successful if you also plan to run sales promotions at the same time. A small, independent music store tried this in November, figuring the period just before the holidays was a good time to have a "25 percent off" promotion. "Absentee" customers were encouraged to use their voucher for any of their sale items (CDs, tapes, videos, etc.) and stock up for the holidays.

Making Contact

From Martin R. Baird

Don't ever let your existing customers fade away. Zero in on your current customers because this is where most of your business will continue to come from. It's much easier to sell to people who have already bought from your company and have been satisfied than it is to seek out sales from new customers. Invite existing customers into your store when you develop new products or when you're offering substantial discounts. Create a database with all your customers' names and addresses so you can keep in touch.

Restaurants are wise practitioners of this strategy. One established Italian restaurant owner wanted to offer something new called "international desserts." She thought it would be a good idea to have a variety of specialty dessert items available for late-night or after-theater dining. She researched what to offer and explored unique ways to present her fare. Then she went to her database, noted who frequently ordered dessert, who frequented the theater, and who loved to travel. She put together a "test batch" of customers to review her ideas and her tasty treats.

Welcome Back, Customers

From Jerry Fisher

Want to get long-lost customers back into your store? Why not send a card to customers you haven't seen in a year telling them they've been missed and that you'd love to see them again? Offer a "welcome back" discount as an incentive. You can give returning customers a dollars-off incentive, a percentage-off offer or any other deal you can think of.

You might even want to take it a step further by trying to determine why those customers left in the first place. If you know they were unhappy about a particular transaction, felt they didn't get proper service, or were disappointed in any other aspect of your business, acknowledge that fact and assure them that the matter has been addressed and corrected. Be sure to offer your incentive along with your apology.

Be A Hero

From Nancy Michaels

Once you've sold your product or service to a client, don't toss his or her name out the window. To build a strong relationship with your customers, stay in contact. Of course, you should notify them when you're having a sale or are introducing something new. But you should also alert customers to seminars or magazine articles they might find relevant. And whenever you think of a way to save clients money or enhance their productivity, let them know. This will help position you as an invaluable resource. You're making them feel they can't do it without you.

The owners of a computer store that had both big and small businesses as clients knew that some of their home-based clients needed to be trained on their particular products before they could really make use of the systems they bought. So whenever they were conducting classes for their larger clients, they would arrange to have a few slots set aside for individuals who couldn't afford a private session to come and learn about their software and hardware. They would do this as a courtesy to the smaller client, and the large company was almost always willing to allow a visitor or two to sit in.

You Gotta Ask

From Diane Perlmutter

Even though it may be a painful process, you need to learn what customers don't like about your product or service. Is your product difficult to use? Is the color obnoxious? Do your customer service reps take too long to field their calls? Make it a point to ask customers what you could be doing better. You'll be surprised how much they appreciate it when you ask for their input. But don't stop there. Once you hear what they have to say, do something with it. That way, you can build the better mousetrap before your competitor does.

For example, if you own an auto body shop, you have ample opportunity to visit a bit with your customers because they'll usually have to come to your shop at least twice—once to drop off and once to pick up. When they stop by and there's a wait, use the time to find out what's important to them. Offer a cup of coffee or a cool drink and ask if they would mind filling out a short questionnaire or answering a survey. Zero in on how the place looks, what your service has been like, and how they liked your work.

Follow The Lead

From Jay Conrad Levinson

Did you know that the difference between a guerrilla and a nonguerrilla is that a nonguerrilla thinks marketing is over once the sale is made? The guerrilla knows that's when marketing begins. The marketing you do subsequent to the sale is where the real profits are, so don't ignore customers once they hand over the cash. Selling to existing customers is easy and inexpensive.

Give yourself a challenge. The next time you acquire a new customer or client, make yourself add one more field to that person's file in your database. Call the category "Next Step." Without locking yourself into anything, try to generate an idea about what you might do for that person down the road. If the purchase involved carpet cleaning, you might want to call in a few weeks and offer to clean the person's upholstered furniture. Throw in a free spot cleaning for the carpets, just to show you like to keep your clients happy and their carpets looking good.

Chapter 7

Expand Your Horizons

Be Territorial

From Al Ries

Expand geographically, not demographically. If you do business with medical doctors in one location, it's easier to find doctors in another community than it is to try to sell to dentists in your home territory. Once you've built a rapport within a certain customer community, your reputation will make it easier for you to sell to like customers in other areas.

If a doctor in Chicago knows that you've sold your product or service to hundreds of doctors in the tri-state area, chances are he or she will place more trust in you than if you've sold only to dentists in a single city. Selling to the same type of customer increases your chances of capitalizing on word-of-mouth marketing and referrals.

Reach Out And
Touch Someone

From Edith Weiner

Trend watchers predict that marketers should pay attention to people with disabilities, as they are becoming a big market. Companies, publications and products and services are emerging to cater to this market. Even if your product or service isn't directly geared to people with disabilities, you can still advertise and market directly to them. And if you can serve some subgroup of that market more effectively than your competitors, you may be able to capture a loyal and lucrative customer base.

One woman who does a lot of seminars and training makes sure she offers her disabled customers something her competitors don't. She's found that her topics seem to be of special interest to people with hearing disabilities, so she's made it a point to have a sign-language interpreter available at her presentations. The word has spread, business has increased, and she's won additional respect from her hearing audience for her efforts.

81

Branch Out

From Al Ries

Who says you have to stick with a single product or service? If you're looking for more customers, launch a second brand. When you run out of potential new customers, do as Toyota did with Lexus—launch a new brand that appeals to customers you aren't presently attracting. This can open the door to a totally different market. If you can make slight changes in your product or service that would make it appeal to a different market, you gain new customers without spending a lot.

A company that specializes in custom cakes for all occasions realized it was missing out on a large market when one of the owner's parents developed diabetes. Suddenly, the owner was aware of how few "sweets" were sugar-free or suited to someone on a restricted diet. So she and her partner started a new line of sugar-free desserts and candies.

One To Grow On

From Michel Roux

It takes time and care to bring your vision to fruition. A lot of companies are growing by acquisition, but this sometimes scatters your focus and takes away from your own products. Try considering organic growth—growing by nurturing your product. By focusing on your own product, you'll discover new markets and, eventually, natural product extensions. Your company will grow in a much more seamless way where all your products, services and markets feed off each other.

One fellow who owns a business that cuts and supplies firewood for hotels and condominiums in the mountains saw potential during the warm summer months to keep in touch with his clients and make some additional money as well. He made an offer to his customers that if they would buy mulch (which he produced from leftover pieces of wood) for their landscaping during the spring and summer, he would give them 20 percent off their firewood orders from October through December. This kept him and his crew busy all year, and he didn't have to lay off employees. This saved him time, too, because he didn't have to rehire and retrain employees in the fall.

Go On A Niche Hunt

From Danielle Kennedy

Go beyond single-niche marketing. Don't get attached to one segment of the marketplace just because it's bringing in profits right now. Develop several niches. Remember that the economy is constantly in flux and that the customers who are bringing in the most revenues for your company today may not be your best customers in the future. By catering to several niche markets, you can avoid disaster if your main market disappears.

This concept can be seen every day in the service sector. A woman who had spent several years training others on how to handle telephone contacts and take messages foresaw that the wave of the future was in high-tech communications. She adapted her format to move from traditional methods to incorporating voice mail, pagers, cell phones and e-mail. Without abandoning what she had done for years, she scaled it down and moved on to what was on the horizon, thereby catering to several niches.

Variety Is The Spice Of Life

From Tim Girvin

Expand your offerings. A successful product array can include variations on a theme. Consider smaller or larger versions of your existing products. For example, the Mag-Lite flashlight comes in sizes ranging from a key-chain model to a policeman's truncheon in scale. By offering a variety of options, you increase the number of potential buyers in two ways: You can reach people who wouldn't have considered buying your original product but who like the variations, and you can turn a single purchase into multiple purchases.

A small Midwestern company that manufactures bird seed took this idea to heart and moved from offering a basic mix to specialized combinations blended especially for particular regions. The owners also packaged their mix in a wide variety of sizes and set up a choice of delivery options.

Whatever It Takes

From Nancy Michaels

Expand your services or product line to meet the growing needs of your customers. As you become more familiar with your clients' needs, you can begin to incorporate some of those new products or services into your business so your customers don't have to go elsewhere. By making your business a sort of one-stop shopping area, you increase sales and strengthen your ties with customers. The more things you offer, the longer they'll linger in your store and the more likely they'll find something that fits their needs.

For instance, look at full-service hair salons and day spas that offer hair, skin and nail-care products. While clients wait for their appointment, they can purchase hair spray, nail polish and moisturizer. The key here, however, is to make sure that what you offer actually relates to your original concept. In other words, hair and beauty supplies are a natural spin-off from the basic salon, but getting into clothing, jewelry and hats may be just a bit much.

Chapter 8

Pass
The Word

Positively Speaking

From Edith Weiner

Marketing experts warn us to beware of the negative. Make sure you deal with all your customers in good faith and with integrity. A single disgruntled customer can do some serious damage to your reputation. Negative word-of-mouth, especially on computer bulletin boards and the Internet, can cripple your business even more than positive public relations can help it. So do things right from the get-go and treat customers with respect.

Take, for example, the contractor whose specialty was pouring concrete driveways. The job he did for one home-owner was second-rate, and when the owner complained, the contractor basically said, "It's down, and it stays the way it is." Want to bet how long it took not only for the customer's family and friends to hear about it but also the whole neighborhood? The contractor would have been wise to happily replace the driveway and make a fairly splashy show of what he was doing, which might have led to several more jobs in that new development.

Talk Of
The Town

From Danielle Kennedy

Word-of-mouth is one of the best—and cheapest—marketing methods on the planet. One way to effectively get the word out is to spread good rumors about yourself and your business. Deliver quality, charge reasonable rates, finish projects before deadline and treat all your customers with respect. In other words, give customers a reason to talk you up to their friends. Encourage them to do so by offering rewards for referrals.

That's exactly what one small sporting goods store that caters to the soccer crowd did. It had received a goodwill award for suppling equipment for an after-school soccer program. The store staff took lots of photos with the kids who were involved and put a display in the store along with the award. They also talked up the fact that they were willing to partner with other groups to help promote the sport. Word spread like wildfire, and profits went up accordingly.

Star Search

From Nancy Michaels

Star treatment isn't just for people in the movies. You can also make your clients the stars of your business. People love to be recognized and appreciated for their patronage. With their permission, why not hang your customers' photos in your place of business? Or feature clients in your company's newsletter? You can be sure that the featured clients will pass the word about their appearance to friends, family and business associates. That helps spread the word about your business at the same time. The ties you create by making customers feel like they're a part of your organization are stronger than any sales pitch or brochure, and they don't cost anything.

You might want to take the lead from a small company in the West that sells farm equipment. Each month it features an "Agribusiness Family Spotlight" in the local newspapers. The ad profiles a family and illustrates why agribusiness is important to us all. The company has really made friends with this campaign—and who knows how many new customers.

Let Customers
Do The Talking

From Rick Crandall

Try collecting testimonials from your customers. Either send them a follow-up questionnaire where they can write in comments, or call customers following a sale and ask a few quick questions. Ask if you can use their comments in your marketing materials—this will flatter them and will help you tremendously. People respond to testimonials from others in their industry or someone in their particular circumstance. Once you know a prospect's needs, you can whip out your file and share the testimonial that best mirrors his or her need.

In addition, this process of collecting testimonials is another good way to do on-the-spot market research. You'll learn lots by asking for feedback, and this affords you a way of keeping in touch with your customer base. Just calling for a "testimonial update" is a sure way of staying connected to your clients.

Chapter 9

Mad
About Ads

Radio Days

From Al Ries

Looking for ways to advertise? How about radio? It's an inexpensive medium (in terms of costs per prospect reached), and it's also inexpensive in terms of production costs—which can be nothing if station announcers read your copy. Do some investigating to determine which radio stations make the most sense in terms of reaching your target market. If your target market is 18- to 24-year-olds, you might want to try the local alternative radio station. If your customers are in the 50-plus age group, think about a news-oriented or classical music station. Stations do extensive research on their demographics, so find one that fits your market.

Also pay attention to the changing tastes of your clientele. Just because you think you know what they listen to now doesn't mean they won't change their minds. Note whether new stations have emerged in your listening area. Sometimes a hot new station will lure listeners away from their favorite stations. Stay tuned in yourself to what your customers are listening to. Remember, surveys and quick questionnaires can give you great insight into your customers' listening habits.

91

Make It Appealing

From Philip Nulman

Finding the right marketing and advertising strategy depends on the kind of product you sell and what it is about that product that makes people want to buy it. Frequently, you can boil it down to two things: emotion or reason. Which sells your business better? Which side of the brain does your business appeal to? Sell motorcycles, and you need an emotional/romantic sales campaign. Sell business forms, and you must appeal to reason. Know the appeal of your business, and make sure your advertising suits it.

One developer working on promoting a collection of homes located near a lake wanted to emphasize how peaceful the location was. His ads, therefore, had the gentle background noises of birds chirping and water lapping the shore. He wasn't just selling his homes—he was offering a way of life.

Join The Crowd

From Diane Perlmutter

When it comes to marketing, it's simple—you need to be where your customers are. In evaluating media, promotional opportunities or sponsorships, try selecting those that reach the highest percentage of your target audience, not just those that deliver the most people. Sure, it may sound great that millions of people will see your ad if you air it during prime time, but if most of those viewers don't fit your target demographic, then you're wasting a bundle. In marketing, smart spending means spending on your target market. Remember, quality is more important than quantity.

For instance, if you own a quick-lube station and one of the advantages you tout is how fast and easy it is to pull in on your way home from work, then your ads should probably run when commuter traffic is at its highest. You might have to pay a bit more for prime "drive time" spots, but your target market will be getting an earful.

Get In The Mix

From Philip Nulman

Smart marketers mix media instead of targeting a single marketing venue. If you communicate using a variety of media (print, broadcast, outdoor, transit), you reach more people and have more chances to reinforce your marketing message. If a consumer hears your ad on the radio, then sees a billboard with your ad, it strengthens your message and increases brand awareness. Examine available media, then develop a plan to reach the most people in different environments for the lowest cost.

One independent jewelry store used this method to promote its Valentine's Day assortment of gemstones. In a well-orchestrated campaign, the name of the store, its owner's picture and samples of beautiful jewelry seemed to pop up everywhere. Since Valentine's Day is a major sales day for jewelry, the owner took almost one-fourth of his advertising budget to blitz the market with his message.

94

Overnight Success

From Jerry Fisher

People get so much mail these days that you really need to grab their attention if you want them to open your direct-marketing pieces. Send out a price-reduction notice in an envelope that looks like it's for overnight delivery. People tend to open overnight packages first, so your ad has a better chance of getting a look instead of heading right for the trash.

Ask your printer about envelope prices—they're much cheaper than you (or your customers) suspect. Then come up with a message that ties in with the "urgent" appeal that an overnight envelope suggests. You might even host a "midnight madness" event that's totally out of character for your company. Tempt your reader with "You've no idea what goes on overnight at Mostly Mozart!"

Have Some Fun

From Philip Nulman

Consumers are bombarded with so many ads, brochures and direct-mail pieces that it's easy for marketing materials to fall through the cracks. Want to keep your messages from bombing? Just remember, sometimes *clever* is better. Develop ads that use creativity to break through the information clutter. But make sure your humor is really funny. You might think something is a knee-slapper, but if your customers don't, your ad will fail miserably. Have several people review your ad before committing it to print. And make sure everything your ads say can be substantiated—or your campaign may backfire.

A great example of a funny, frisky ad campaign that didn't backfire came from the collaborative efforts of an ad agency in Florida and a small company in Texas. The company manufactures a new line of colognes created just for our canine pals. One of the print ads that was created read "Strong enough for a man, but made for a Chihuahua." A good laugh was had by all, and the ads certainly got the readers' attention.

96

Give 'Em Their Lumps

From Jerry Fisher

Want a sure-fire way to get your customers to open your direct-mail piece? Try this technique that nobody can resist: Customers will always open an envelope with a lump in it or a small box of anything. Put a swatch or sample of a new product you want to promote inside an envelope. Obviously, some products just can't be squeezed in, but don't worry. Just include something that relates to your product or something that you can play off of in a product announcement. For instance, a note saying "If you want to test the new phone system, just whistle" could accompany a bright, shiny whistle.

97

Media Mixer

From Jay Conrad Levinson

Marketing isn't just traditional advertising, or direct mail or telemarketing. It's a combination of weapons—a wide assortment that you deploy systematically. And these days, that includes being comfortable with technology, especially the Internet. Targeting the Internet in addition to other marketing avenues can only strengthen your battle to win market share.

Take the lead from some of your favorite Web sites. Or simply ask friends or colleagues what they do to advertise on the Internet. If they are happy with their efforts, ask who helped them get started and then go to those people for assistance. Get to know how to use all the latest marketing weapons at your disposal because the wider your weapon selection, the wider the grin on your face when you review your profits.

Infomercial Info

From Jerry Fisher

The old two-for-one offer still works. Up your infomercial response rate by always offering a second item free with a purchase. This doesn't mean you have to cut your profits in half—the freebie item can be of a much lower value than the purchased product. Even if the give-away item is of a nominal value, this technique can turn fence sitters into buyers.

A company that specializes in Cajun spices and cooking ingredients has a lively, creative infomercial and also advertises in select cable TV slots. When someone makes a purchase, the company sends along a CD of Cajun music. You can hear it playing in the background of the TV spots. It's a great way to jazz up the message and get people feeling good about the company's line of ingredients.

Ex-Marketing

From Philip Nulman

Contrary to popular belief, your company doesn't have to be everything to all people. Sometimes it's just as important to let customers know what you *don't* carry, as well as what you *do* carry, and to let people know who you *aren't* targeting, as well as who you *are* targeting. To do so, create exclusionary messages.

For instance, a gourmet shop might brag "No Silly Cereals Here!" That plays up the fact that you will find only gourmet items and unusual ingredients in the store. By excluding certain customers, the owners are actually strengthening their unique selling position.

100

Sell After The Sale

From Jerry Fisher

The infomercial aftermarket can prove very profitable if you take advantage of it. Never produce an infomercial for the primary sale alone. For every one unit sold via television, 10 can sell via retail with the label "As Seen on TV"—so make sure you put those labels on everything shown in infomercials. Another infomercial after-sale tactic: Follow up with TV buyers by sending an updated brochure of your entire line whenever you introduce a new product.

This approach works well for one company that sells exercise equipment through infomercials. Whenever someone calls to order a piece of equipment (or even to inquire about it), the person's name goes into a database with a flag indicating that it requires follow-up. Usually, this means a catalog of workout clothing and small equipment is sent to the caller. The theory here is "Why not look good on your way to feeling good?"

101

If It Worked Once, It'll Work Again

From Al Ries

Much of good marketing is simple and based on common sense. Basically, you just do more of what has worked. Find out what marketing strategies have worked best for your company, then go out and do more of that— while doing less of what hasn't worked.

To know what works and what doesn't, you'll need to devise a tracking system. For instance, if you are placing a coupon in two local mailers, put an identifying mark on the coupons so when customers redeem them, you'll know which mailer they came from. The marks don't have to be complicated. In fact, if you're printing thousands, you can save money simply by printing half on one color of paper and the other half on a different color. If one of the mailers pulls much better than the other, concentrate your coupon efforts on that one and eliminate the other.

102

Take The Test

From Rick Crandall

One of the most important rules of marketing is test, test, test. Always do marketing test runs before you commit cash to an advertising campaign. Before you send out a mailing, run it by a few people. Before you commit to a Yellow Pages ad, test it on a flier. Before you go crazy with any ad, test it on a smaller scale.

Let's say you want to see how an ad campaign for your pet store will fly. Maybe you'll be carrying a completely organic, nonpreservative line of pet food. Send sample fliers to some of your best customers, then a few days later call your customers personally to get their feedback. Or put a voice-mail message on your answering system announcing the new product line. Ask callers to share their reaction to the recorded message.

103

Know Your Measurements

From Jay Conrad Levinson

You should use a lot of marketing weapons, but realize that some will hit the bull's-eye while others will miss the target. A popular and proven method of marketing comes via a business reply card inserted in specifically targeted magazines. But how will you know which reply cards are effective and which ones aren't? By tracking your responses to measure the effectiveness of your weaponry.

For instance, if you are running a business reply card in two magazines, insert codes on each of them so that when the responses come in, you'll know which magazine they came from. Include requests such as "Ask for Department A" in classified ads and "Ask for Department B" in fliers you distribute locally.

And, of course, don't forget that you can always ask customers directly how they found out about your business. Just be certain that you have a system in place ahead of time to track and measure results no matter what your marketing campaign entails. The time to figure out a way to tally the score is not during the middle of the game.

104

Make The Most Of Your Mistakes

From Peter Connolly

Have you considered the value of learning from your mistakes? To break new ground, you might have to handle a few slip-ups. Few mistakes are catastrophic, unless we don't learn from them. Take a good, hard look at what went wrong and do your best to fix the problem. Wrong advertising medium? Switch to another. Bad timing on a sale? Reschedule. Sometimes a minor snafu can lead to a major success if you learn from your mistake.

Case in point: The owner of a brand-new wine and spirits store thought he had turned over every rock looking for hazards that might affect the success of his business. He knew there was a market for his products and decided to locate in an upscale new shopping center at the corner of a very busy intersection. The problem? He failed to check out what the highway department's plans were for access to and from the center. Unfortunately, the entrance and exit streets made for an awkward approach to his store and ultimately cost him a lot of business. You can bet next time he'll check things like access and traffic flow.

Chapter 10

Be The
Expert

105

The Write Stuff

From Al Ries

Offer to write an article on your field for a newspaper or magazine. Even if you write the article for free, you can still make some money in the deal. Here's how: It can bring you valuable inquiries from prospects who see the story. It improves your image as an expert in the field and builds credibility. Be sure to get reprints of any articles you write and include them in your sales materials.

In fact, to make the most of your chance to have something printed, look ahead to what holidays, special events or key deadlines (like tax time) are coming up. Make yourself available as an expert, and have your article already developed so it's easy to get the information to the right source. For example, if you own a company that coordinates parties and special events, the time to offer your services as an expert resource is right before the holidays. Suggest an article on appropriate business gifts or things to consider when the company holiday party rolls around.

106

Speak Up!

From Martin R. Baird

One of the best ways to market your product or service is to speak at community events. Offering your expertise at a public occasion is an easy way to get the word out about your business without having it sound like a sales pitch. You'll maximize your impact, while lending credibility to your product or service. You'll be surprised how many customers will surface following a speaking engagement.

Follow this lead: An acupuncturist offered to do an informational program on the myths and magic of acupuncture. She contacted a number of service clubs and social organizations, knowing full well how hard it is to come up with a program week after week. But she made sure she had a quality presentation to offer and that she was highly professional and entertaining in her delivery.

107

Tip Sheet

From Rick Crandall

Create a handout of handy tips. A landscaper could compile 10 ways to prepare a lawn for fall; a lawyer might list 10 ways to avoid going to court. Use these tips in seminars, brochures, ads or press releases. Hand them out at trade shows or other events where you'll find consumers. The tips establish your expertise; giving them away creates gratitude in potential customers.

You might even go so far as to print a few tips on the back of a business card. If your service or product line is suited to this approach, then think about having cards designed that allow you to be of service in two ways—your name and address, plus a valuable piece of information to carry along.

108

Big News

From Nancy Michaels

One of the most effective ways of maintaining virility is through writing. If you don't already send a company newsletter to clients, consider doing so. Include information about yourself, upcoming sales, new products and services, employees, industry changes and more. Offer tips on how to use your company's products or services better and offer advice on topics of interest to your audience. In addition to circulating your own newsletter, offer to write articles in industry publications your clients read.

A favorite approach for a couple who own a landscape nursery is to do a "Time To . . ." newsletter. They make a point of reminding readers when it's time to fertilize roses, prune lilacs, plant bulbs and so on. They also take a philosophical look at taking time to stop and smell the roses during our busy and hectic lives. It's a nice combination of information and care-taking.

109

Screen Test

From Jerry Fisher

Videos can make you a star in the prospect's eye. Whatever your area of expertise, create a video with 10 tips that can help your customers. Offer the video free of charge if a client signs up to use your service for a trial period, or use the video as a marketing device to entice customers to give your service a try.

For instance, a real estate investment company purporting to offer land that has appreciated in value an average of 25 percent annually could provide clients with a free, provocatively titled video just for the opportunity to sit down and discuss its properties with a potential customer. The title: "10 Golden Rules for Picking Investments That Appreciate Over 25 Percent a Year." It sounds a little too good to be true but enough within the realm of possibility to draw a response.

110

Chair Lift

From Danielle Kennedy

Two ways to make a name for yourself in your industry are to attend trade association functions and to chair events. As an active member of your industry's trade association, you'll build credibility with customers and create opportunities for strategic alliances through networking. You may have to eat your share of rubber chickens, but when you chair committees for your trade association, you meet important people in your industry and exchange ideas and leads. The next thing you know, referrals will come to your door from three states over.

This can be a unexpected windfall, according to one fellow who owns a company that cleans and recycles dirty oil that's been used in machinery or cars. While he was chairing a committee to develop the program for a recycling conference, he was approached by a large paving company that wanted him to handle the cleaning of the oil products it used in its heavy equipment. No one had to drill him for a response.

111

Get In The Know

From Jerry Fisher

Offer helpful consumer information to your customers. It enhances your image as an expert and makes customers feel like they're getting a better value. When you provide detailed and personalized information, it also gives clients the impression that you care about them.

For example, buyers of vitamin, mineral and herb supplements are faced with so many choices that they may have a hard time deciding what to take. A marketer of supplements might offer to create a customized regimen for each prospect who completes a questionnaire about health complaints, lifestyle and other data. In return, the recipient agrees to buy from the company and subscribe to its newsletter.

112

On Board

From Nancy Michaels

Lend your expertise to your clients. If a client has an informal panel of advisors, offer to join. One of the problems for people who work independently or have small businesses is that they don't have enough people to use as sounding boards. By acting as an expert, you'll send your credibility soaring and you'll make solid contacts with other advisors. Creating a similar panel for your own business is also good practice.

The owner of a dinner theater took this step and asked a number of patrons and business leaders in her community to serve on an advisory board. Their input was invaluable, and since she wasn't able to compensate them monetarily, she provided great seats to any show they wanted to see. The trade-off worked well for the board members and their guests, plus it brought new people to the theater.

113

Dear Editor . . .

From Rick Crandall

When you read an article that pertains to your field, write a letter to the editor. Offer more information that will benefit readers or note any errors that appeared in the story. This is a relatively easy thing to do, and it provides prime exposure in the publications that your target audience reads. Always include your name and company contact information, and make sure to note that you own the company. The publication will most likely include this information with your signature, which will allow readers to get in touch with you.

Chapter 11

Be Your Own Best Ad

114

Back To School

From Danielle Kennedy

Your business can only be as good as you are, so you need to work harder on yourself than on your business. That means you should continually go to school and learn. This effort doesn't necessarily have to be on the scale of enrolling in an MBA program at a prestigious university. It could entail something as simple as sharpening your writing skills for business letters, or brushing up on your phone etiquette. Staying up to date on new technology may also keep you one step ahead of the competition.

One woman who owns a small store that handles all kinds of shipping and packing needs made it her goal to stay informed regarding domestic and international shipping regulations. She is on the Internet frequently, updating her own database so that when that certain someone comes into her store and asks about the policy for shipping food items to New Zealand, she has at her fingertips at least some applicable information. It sure makes her look like a bona fide expert in the eyes of her customers, and it has her competition green with envy.

115

Don't Forget The Little People

From Guy Kawasaki

Learn how to "suck down." That's right. All "strategic" plans aside, getting new business often comes down to whether one secretary likes you or not. If you're rude to Mr. Big's assistant, you risk getting stuck in the "Sorry, he's in a meeting" zone. Be cordial to everyone you deal with—secretaries, receptionists, assistants, doormen, etc.

People who are in sales are well aware of how important this rule is. A fellow who covers a broad territory for his products never makes a stop without leaving something with the secretary or receptionist. He makes notes about what their kids are doing, where they took their last vacation, and what their new car looks like. Remember, sucking up changes the color of your nose; sucking down changes the color of your balance sheet.

116

Be Confident

From Jay Conrad Levinson

In a study of 10,000 people designed to determine why folks patronize the businesses they do, price came in fifth, selection fourth, service third and quality second. The No. 1 factor? People said they patronize businesses they have confidence in. Your commitment will make them confident; so will your consistency. And if they're confident, they're customers.

Some women who own a small travel agency in the Southwest have demonstrated their commitment to their clients so often that people refer to them as the "snoop sisters." They will go to the ends of the earth looking for the best travel packages for their clients. They investigate every angle and resource before finalizing itineraries and try to personally visit as many of the properties and locations as possible. Why? Because they want their customers to feel absolute confidence in the arrangements and accommodations that have been booked for them.

117

What's The Big Deal?

From Dan Peña

In the business world, you're measured by transactions, not income. Unless you're a rock star or a sports celebrity, you're never going to get rich by being paid an income. You get rich or increase your wealth primarily through share and equity deals. People who are supersuccessful are measured by the deals they've done, not by the income they've created off any one deal. A great marketing strategy is to do as many deals as possible—even if, in some cases, you don't make any money on them. The more deals you close, the more people will look to you when they need to make a deal.

Consider the fellow who loves organizing fishing excursions to the wilderness area where he grew up. Sometimes he didn't make a dime on a trip, but he had a dozen guests who were raving afterward about the most fabulous outing they'd ever had. He rarely turned away requests and tried to make something work for almost everyone who inquired. He could see deals in the making and so could his clientele. Their satisfaction sold the concept to others because everyone saw the high level of experience the owner acquired after organizing some 90 trips.

118

Wow!

From Jay Conrad Levinson

There are things about your business that you take for granted but that would amaze your customers and prospects if they knew. The easiest way to find out just what it is about your business that wows people is to talk it up. When you meet someone and talk about your business, take note of what gets the biggest reaction. Be sure all your marketing efforts include an element of amazement—to attract attention, and even to obtain free public relations.

A married couple who own a large, independent printing business often let it be known how many millions of pages they printed each year, or how challenging it was bringing a million-dollar press from Germany to their little hometown in the States. When people hear about the volume they do and the effort it took to get such a sophisticated press set up and running, they never forget that printing company.

119

Strong Medicine

From Peter Connolly

Can you believe there is actually an army of marketing experts out there who want you to be a quitter? It's true—only what they want you to give up is that constant worrying about your weaknesses. Play off your strongest attributes and focus on your strengths. Emphasize in your advertising and marketing what you do best. This will help consumers understand what you stand for and why you're better than the competition. However, be certain the brand strengths you identify are meaningful and relevant to your customers.

Take, for example, the man who owns a custom hat shop in the Rocky Mountains. He says right in his brochure and in his ads that he doesn't have anything to offer that other hat makers don't have, except his keen eye and trained hand. He says he's been at this business for 44 years, has seen how hats should be shaped and can feel a flaw instantly.

120

Success Stories

From Dan Peña

Promote yourself based on your successes and on those of others. Several years back, I was the subject of a Pulitzer Prize-winning *Los Angeles Times* newspaper article. I'm still riding that prize—though its legs are about half worn off by now. And even though I didn't *earn* the prize, I benefited from my association with it.

Madonna is another example of someone who markets herself in this fashion. Follow her lead and promote your business by emphasizing your associations with other successful businesses, events and people. The more you can surround your business with success, the more you will be viewed as successful, and the more successful you will become.

A catering company located in the same city as a major PGA tournament highlighted the fact that it had been chosen to handle all the food and beverages for the players' hospitality tent for the past three years. It made a big deal of how prestigious this was and even used some photos taken with the pro golfers in its promo pieces.

121

Do The Old Soft Shoe

From Nancy Michaels

Don't hard sell potential customers. If clients feel you're only trying to get more out of them to make a sale, and you're not really coming to them with solutions or ideas, that leaves a sour taste in their mouths. Instead of going for broke with first-time buyers, think long term. Even if you make less money than usual off that first sale, you'll make it up in repeat business.

Consider a couple who own a security alarm service. They made a call on a prospective client who was building a new manufacturing plant. The couple, of course, wanted to install their system in the entire facility, but realized they were new to the area and there were several others competing for the bid. Instead of jumping in headfirst, they just stuck their toes in the water by asking to install one of their most innovative, unobtrusive systems in the annex building adjacent to the main plant. They gave the owner a great price and superb service, plus he got firsthand knowledge of their system in advance of making his decision for the new plant.

Chapter **12**

Get
Wired

122

Techno-Talk

From Guy Kawasaki

et personal with technology. No, this isn't a contra-diction in terms. E-mail, Web sites and listservs enable you to maintain close contact with a lot of people, including customers and vendors, at a very low cost. And often it's easier and quicker to get information from a Web site or through e-mail than by playing telephone tag.

Let's say you own a company that specializes in selling imported and microbrewed beers directly to the consumer. Often you get special promotional deals from brewers themselves. Wouldn't it be a nice surprise to share this good news with some of your key customers who are especially fond of the particular brands involved? Through technology, you can set up your own database so that when certain customer profiles match the offers that are available, you can instantly let them know about the savings they might enjoy by sending them e-mail messages or posting a special announcement on your Web page.

123

Don't Get Caught In The Web

From Bruce Judson

Don't create a Web site just because it's the thing to do. Decide why you're building your site and design it with this in mind. You should have a clear objective before you start; otherwise you'll end up spending thousands of dollars for a site that doesn't meet your needs. But don't limit yourself—Web sites can serve a number of goals: You can advertise, sell, build prospect lists or experiment with hundreds of other ideas.

One company in the Northwest that provides therapeutic equipment for swimming pools had a very limited market for several years until its owner realized he could target specific rehabilitation and hospital organizations via a Web site. The company now advertises, acts as a resource, and helps provide connections for all sorts of groups that need its special therapeutic equipment.

124

Bits And Bytes

From Bruce Judson

The Web is a new medium, so you don't have gobs of success stories (or failures, for that matter) to look to for guidance. So what do you do? Learn through experience. Start by experimenting with a small site and make changes as needed. It's far more important to get a site going than to spend months planning it.

Many small businesses find that they can get started safely, quickly and inexpensively by participating in an organizational directory that appears on the Web. For example, a variety of businesses can be listed and have their own Web sites simply by joining the local chamber of commerce. In most cases, as a chamber member, your business appears as part of the online directory, and your site could consist of one simple page. It's a great way to get started and give yourself some time to grow.

125

Web Mail

From Bruce Judson

ere's another great tip for your Web site. Ask if visitors to your site want to be notified about new products and services or special sales. It's easy—and cheap—to gather the names and addresses (e-mail and snail mail) of visitors who want to hear more about specific new products or services. You can also use this list to create a database of names to which you can send postcards, brochures and other mailings. Or tap into your database to ask for simple demographic information to add to your market research efforts.

A woman who owns a candle shop started her very successful birthday club this way. As people visit her Web site, she asks them simply to enter their birth date. When that special day rolls around, they automatically receive a coupon good for 50 percent off their next candle purchase.

126

Web Site Unseen

From Bruce Judson

Interactive marketing is still so young that no one knows what will and will not work. As a result, you'll want to occasionally change your site (no matter how well-planned it may be) based on what you learn from operating it. Usually, that will require extra capital. Even if your efforts on the Web work just fine, you'll still need to freshen up your site from time to time to keep viewers coming back. You should budget money upfront for updates so you won't be caught by surprise.

For instance, let's say you offer a variety of automotive parts and accessories for vintage cars. You may find that a particular line of waxes and finish protectors starts to sell extremely well. If you've planned ahead, you can afford to expand what you have to offer in that line by adding pages to your Web site.

127

Let's Talk About Tech

From Watts Wacker

Technology's influence in our lives is becoming emotional and persuasive. We are no longer afraid of technology; we have mastered it as a new way of communicating. When you think of a friend after reading a commentary in the newspaper, for example, instead of phoning, you'll fax the article. Or you'll read something on the Web and immediately download it and e-mail it to your friend. Technology has become intricately woven into our daily lives at all levels: business, personal and emotional. Keep that in mind when you're looking for ways to use technology in your marketing.

One fellow who provides data management and billing services for a variety of small to midsized businesses made note of a conversation he had with one of his customers. It seemed she was an amateur astronomer and very interested in telescopes. So when he ran across an article in one of his favorite magazines about an exhibit on telescopes that was coming to a local museum, he faxed a copy to his customer, along with a short note. What a great way to let someone see how truly personal his service could be.

128

Net Works

From Bruce Judson

If you have a broad product line, offer a referral service on your Web site. Ask visitors to your site to provide information about their needs. In this way, you can program your Web site to recommend appropriate products. By sorting through options and finding the right choice for each visitor, you provide value to these potential customers. You may also want to program your site so that if a customer orders a certain type of product, say, herbal teas, the Web site will automatically direct him or her to other complementary products you offer, such as natural vitamins or food supplements. This can boost sales without costing you a dime.

129

Web Alert

From Bruce Judson

One factor is often overlooked by people just getting started with a Web site: They fail to promote their site everywhere. Include Web addresses on all packaging and in all print and broadcast advertising. Also include your address on all written communications: letterhead, business cards, envelopes, marketing brochures and fliers. Consider buying Web-based advertising that leads prospects directly to your site. Use "action" ads where one click on the ad transports the user to your home page. Even better, if you offer reciprocal links to noncompetitors who attract the same demographic you are seeking, that can increase traffic to your site for free.

A good example of reciprocal links comes from a business that makes and sells sealant for redwood decks and furniture. The sealant company linked up with a lumberyard and a business that manufactures redwood patio furniture.

130

Search And Seizure

From Bruce Judson

To make sure people can find your Web site, try registering with Internet search engines. The Internet has many indexes that send people to sites related to particular topics. For instance, there's Yahoo! (www.yahoo.com), Lycos (www.lycos.com), Infoseek (www.infoseek.com), WebCrawler (webcrawler.com) and Excite (www. excite.com). Some search engines allow you to register in various categories, so before signing up, think about the categories where it would make sense to list your company's site—fitness, education, travel, etc.—and come up with a short (most search engines allow only 25 words or less) and snappy description of your company and your site. Register your site with as many engines as you can find. If you don't have the time to do it yourself, there are Internet marketing companies that will register your site for you—for a fee, of course.

131

1-800-Web-Site

From Bruce Judson

A Web site may cost thousands of dollars to design, but it can wire you for some large cost savings in the future. Just think: A toll-free number for taking orders or customer service costs about $1 per minute. If customers communicate with you through the Web, these costs are eliminated entirely, and the savings go directly to the bottom line. That means your Web site could pay for itself within a very short time period.

Take, for example, a company that supplies thousands of gardeners with their bulbs for spring planting. If every toll-free call lasts an average of six minutes, an order would have to amount to at least $24 to generate an adequate profit for the supplier. But with an Internet order, there is no upfront cost, so even small orders are very profitable.

132

Keep It Simple

From Bruce Judson

Listen to your best salesperson pitch your product or service. The essence of what he or she says is the basis for a great Web site. After all, just like a sales pitch, your Web site should include lots of information about the benefits of your products or services. Don't get caught up in a bunch of techno mumbo jumbo. Keep it simple and to the point. Since putting marketing materials on the Web doesn't involve the same costs as printing on paper stock, some business owners go crazy online, putting far more information than anyone would ever want or need. If you do, your customers will go to another site that's more user friendly.

In fact, try to remember the rules of any good marketing piece. Make it as easy to understand and as painless to follow as possible. If you are promoting your services as a cracker-jack auctioneer for estate furniture, then list with bullets the key factors and past experience that make you the best. In less than a minute, a visitor should be able to get a sense of what makes you special.

133

Sites For Sore Eyes

From Bruce Judson

More than 5,000 new commercial Web sites pop up every month, so how do you make users click on your site? Well, here's one answer: Recognize that you are competing for an audience the same way you compete for attention in more traditional arenas. To make it online, you need to develop a promotional plan. A "Field of Dreams" strategy (build it, and they will come) doesn't work.

If you want people to visit your "Everything Billiards" Web site, start by researching what is already available. See what your competition is doing and get a feel for where you must be seen. Then explore the various links that make sense for you and the sites that potential customers might visit. Find out what the costs will be for design, placement and fulfillment. Then start spending those advertising dollars.

134

www. YourNameHere

From Jay Conrad Levinson

Choose a name for your Web site carefully. The name of your site is extremely important. Don't try to get fancy or cutesy. You should stick with names that are easy to remember and spell. If the name of your company is short enough and it gives a good indication of what type of business you're in, use that. It will reinforce name recognition.

In addition, when naming a business, follow common sense rules like choosing a name that's easy to pronounce. If people can't pronounce your name, they will probably avoid visiting your site. And try to choose a name that's meaningful to the customers you're trying to attract. If it is so cryptic or highly specialized that only a handful of visitors can understand what it is you do or provide, then you're defeating the purpose behind trying to communicate with as many people as possible. Remember, the more your name communicates initially, the less effort you must exert to explain it, and that means it will be easier to find you in the first place.

135

Yadda, Yadda, Yadda

From Jay Conrad Levinson

There is a growing audience for your marketing message to be found chatting on the Web. Enter online "chat rooms" frequently, and aim to get in on discussions where you can offer advice in your field of expertise. If you're a wedding planner, you may want to tap into chat rooms where brides-to-be are sharing info on how to save money on flowers, caterers and photographers. To build strong relationships that can pay off down the line, strive for one-on-one interactions with Web users.

136

By The Bookmark

From Jay Conrad Levinson

On the Web, content is king. Keep in mind that better content makes for a better Web site. Never compromise on the quality of your content—that's what draws people in. You've got to offer them some information they can use. If you sell fitness products on the Web, don't just present your products—offer 10 workout tips. If you own a restaurant and you accept take-out orders on the Web, post a recipe of the day from your menu. If you add some data and some fun content, people will be more likely to bookmark your site.

One woman even offers a daily tip on how to care for pets. She owns a pet shop and obedience training school for every sort of critter from Fido to potbellied pigs. Her pet tips cover a range of subjects and are always funny or entertaining, as well as valuable. From anacondas to zebras, she always finds something relevant to post on her page.

137

Easy Does It

From Jay Conrad Levinson

One of the most common mistakes people make when marketing online is using techniques that come across as pushy. The Internet is a pretty cool medium where members appreciate a delicate touch. Forget the heavy-handed tactics and put on the soft sell. The more low-key your approach, the better it will be received. Couch your pitch with info that will benefit viewers.

Consider, for instance, the Virtual Florist Web site. It happily and creatively allows you to send a variety of virtual bouquets to anyone you want, and then gently reminds you that it also has the ability to help you with your real flower orders. It can provide delivery service and a choice of floral combinations that are beautifully suited to whatever you need. But the real kick comes in being able to send a virtual bouquet in a matter of seconds to a friend in cyberspace.

138

Coming Soon

From Jay Conrad Levinson

The online world moves at the speed of light, and Web sites can get stale very quickly. Once you create a site, don't think you can just sit back and watch the profits roll in. Viewers need a compelling reason to visit your site more than once. Keep promising something new. Your Web site should constantly promote what's coming up in the near future so users will return again and again. Keep adding to and improving your site from the day you launch it.

A Web site for an Internet service provider has a page featuring a little cartoon chair, table and TV set. Clicking on the TV screen always brings up a surprise message or something interesting to explore. The little TV screen is updated frequently, but at irregular times, just to keep visitors on their toes.

139

Do It
Write

From Jay Conrad Levinson

Web sites, electronic newsletters and e-zines are in constant need of new information and fresh content to entice people to revisit their sites and read their publications. One of the best ways to create an online presence is to e-mail sites and volunteer content on a regular basis. Do this and you will build credibility for your business and cement your position as an expert in your field. Write articles and offer information that would be helpful to potential customers. Always include a bio of yourself with a brief description of your business as well as information on how to reach you.

140

Right Back Atcha

From Jay Conrad Levinson

The Web culture moves much more quickly than the rest of the business world, and people expect immediate results. If visitors to your Web site have questions, reply within a day or two, or you're liable to lose them as customers. Fast response is the single most important factor in retaining Web users. This means setting aside time to check your e-mail and respond to queries several times a day. To respond to the most common requests, prepare form letters that you can simply copy and paste into e-mail.

For instance, let's say you own a building supply company for do-it-yourselfers. Your Web site certainly could promote the variety of materials and tools you offer, but it also could play off the many questions that people have when trying to do a project or repair on their own. A simple page titled "The Doctor is In" could be a place to diagnose the ailments and queries that customers share with you.

141

Get To The Point

From Jay Conrad Levinson

When interacting online, brevity is the rule. People simply will not read lengthy e-mails. If you don't get straight to the point in the first few sentences, you risk having readers delete your mail before they find out about your products and special offers. Learn to express yourself concisely so you don't waste people's time.

It may even be worth your while to acknowledge that people are busy and that your message will not take long to view. In fact, if your product or service is geared to a particular niche, you might even say that upfront. For instance: "If you are hearing impaired, then this service will make a big difference in your quality of life." In other words, let the reader know who the message is really for.

142

Follow-Up Formula

From Jay Conrad Levinson

It's unlikely you'll achieve the results you want from your Web site right away. Try not to be turned off when people don't respond immediately. You need to follow up several times with potential prospects. To keep your company's name in front of customers, send out a weekly newsletter or tip sheet with useful information and include a special offer each week.

To illustrate, let's assume you're promoting your hybrid vegetable seeds. Perhaps you don't get the response you want right away. If that's the case, continue to e-mail your customers and mention the fact that several messages have already been shared. Allude to "Tip #2" and say something like "By now you should be seeing results from that secret to tomato magic." That might be just enough to pique their interest and get them to respond.

143

Hot Links

From Jay Conrad Levinson

The more gateways to other sites you have, the better. Try to find free links, or "trade outs," where you offer a link to someone's site and he or she provides one in return. Many sites are willing to offer links at no cost. In fact, you shouldn't have to pay for links at all. It's possible to offer hundreds of links on your site, but make sure they all appeal to your target audience.

A woman who writes a monthly newsletter for people who love to go fly-fishing has (pardon the pun) hooked up with dozens of other sites that offer everything from custom fly rods to recipes for preparing fish over a campfire.

144

Honor Roll

From Jay Conrad Levinson

Get the word out about your Web site. Try to land your site on "what's new" and "what's cool" lists found on popular sites such as Yahoo! and Netscape. E-mail a pitch letter of no more than three paragraphs explaining why you should be listed. Your Web site really needs to have something extra to make it worthy of being named to these lists—whether it's a cool design element or some really great content—so keep that in mind when you're designing your home page. No matter what kind of company you run, you can create a Web site that's unique and makes a splash. Then build an "honor roll" on your site mentioning all the lists you've graced.

This strategy applies beautifully if you've invented something or have a highly developed skill. A man whose wife became disabled following an accident invented a tool that allows her to reach items that are way beyond her grasp from a wheelchair. This accomplishment was featured in numerous publications and won an achievement award as well. Properly "packaged" and concisely explained, this would be the kind of product that truly answers the questions "What's new?" and "What's cool?"

145

Stay Online

From Jay Conrad Levinson

Just like in traditional marketing, you need to be consistent with your online marketing. Don't expect results if you market your business online only occasionally or haphazardly. You need to maintain a constant presence to build a solid reputation in the online universe. Keeping your name out there will improve awareness of your brand and keep you on top.

And bear in mind that keeping a constant presence means more than the same old message month after month. "Constant" and "up to date" are the bywords for making your online efforts pay off.

146

Be Web Ready

From Leann Anderson

Marketing your Web site in every medium you can is a good practice. In fact, do a little audit of your communications and advertising pieces. See to it that your Web address is included, and if you find some areas where the Web address is missing, make it a priority to get it included as soon as possible.

But remember—whenever you market your Web site via other mediums, you will be fair game for site visits almost immediately. Don't make the same mistake as the small courier service that decided to advertise its Web site in an effort to electronically line up more deliveries and communicate more quickly. The problem? The site started receiving so many hits and orders that the business realized it wasn't prepared to accommodate its customers. The lesson here should be to have your response system finely tuned before you start your ads.

Chapter 13

Be A
Name
Dropper

147

Trade Talks

From Al Ries

When it comes to trade talks, we're not just talking about big business. Small-business owners can do a lot of trading, too. You may think your mailing list is proprietary and should never be shared with anyone else, but it may be one of the best things you can trade. A simple case of "You show me yours, I'll show you mine" can beef up your mailing list with hot prospects. The trick: Find someone who sells a noncompeting product or service to a similar market and swap lists.

Two businesses that shared mailing lists were a lawn care and landscaping company, and a tree spraying and trimming company. While one company certainly saw clients more frequently than the other, the businesses knew most of their customers would have a need for both at some point in time.

148

For Your Eyes Only

From Edith Weiner

Respect your customers' privacy. More than ever, we are living increasingly at the mercy of scam artists, zealous telemarketers, electronic eavesdroppers and massive databanks. The public is becoming increasingly concerned about who is getting, seeing or using private information they may have willingly given to you. If your company routinely sells lists from your customer database, you might want to think about giving customers an option to take their names off the lists you sell. This simple gesture lets the customers feel like they are in control of where their information goes, and they'll appreciate the fact that you have their best needs in mind.

149

Test-Tube Marketing

From Ruth Owades

Direct marketers need to carefully consider the mailing lists they rent—and test them first. The ability to test multiple variables is one of the strongest appeals of direct marketing. By tracking the results, you can tell which lists are the most effective and dump the ones that don't bring in the dollars.

This tracking can be done rather simply at first. Suppose you're an independent financial planner and are looking for more clients. By color-coding your mailing and sending an offer for a free consultation to a sampling of new retirees, parents of young kids, and women between the ages of 25 and 40, you can track which groups respond the best before you do a mass mailing to all three.

150

Names For Sale

From Al Ries

Many marketing experts advocate buying a mailing list to help generate new leads. There's a list available to find new customers for any business, no matter how specialized. A well-targeted mailing is a proven way to find new clients. When shopping for a list, you can make it as general or as specific as you like. However, for each "select," or specification, the more expensive it will be. A list may cost $10 per thousand names, and another $10 per thousand for each select.

For example, let's say you want a list of males (first select) living within 10 miles of Dallas (second select) between the ages of 20 and 29 (third select) who have made a mail order purchase in the past year (fourth select). In this example, the list would end up costing you $50 per thousand names—$10 for the basic list, plus $40 for the four selects.

Chapter 14

Go Public

151

Be A News Hound

From Betty Hoeffner

Want to get some publicity for your business? Then start thinking like a journalist. Think about how issues your business deals with relate to front-page news—such as affirmative action and how it might affect your company or industry—and pitch your story that way. If you can tie your business into a bigger news story, you have a much better chance of seeing your company's name in print than if you send out a tired old press release about how your company is the world's best whatever.

A small company that specializes in putting together "survival kits" for all kinds of groups pitched a story to the education editor of a large newspaper. The angle focused on the kits being assembled for students getting ready to leave for college. Of course, the company sent the information in midsummer so that there was plenty of time to do an article before students left in the fall. A clever black-and-white photo was also included with each press release.

152

Make A Splash

From Jack Trout

Lots of companies come up with terrific ideas but never get anywhere because they don't get into consumers' minds. And even if your company is the first in the marketplace, you may not achieve the success you're hoping for if you ignore your marketing effort. If you don't make any noise, eventually, somebody else gets credit for being first.

Here's a guy who did make a lot of noise. He came up with the idea to manufacture portable storage sheds. The shed is delivered, empty, to your front door. You load it and then call for a pickup truck to come get it and store it in a secure compound. His idea grabbed people because he did plenty of marketing to key niche groups like people preparing to move, college students going home for the summer, and retirees looking to downsize from a home to a condo.

153

No Kidding!

From Betty Hoeffner

When pitching stories to journalists, make sure your story suggestion passes the "No kidding!" test. A journalist's job is to tell his or her readers, listeners or viewers something they didn't know yesterday. If you can make a journalist say "No kidding—I didn't know that," your success rate will be much higher. A press release that contains startling statistics about something relevant to your business, outrageous anecdotes about your business practices, or little-known historical facts about your industry or product can add sparkle to an otherwise dull press release.

A family that owns a dude ranch delights in the fact that six generations of sons have managed the ranch since the 1890s. So when passing on the word about what a terrific vacation or meeting site the ranch can be, they're sure to include both the historical significance of the owners and a few of the romantic stories that go along with life on a ranch.

154

Get In The Fun Zone

From Rick Crandall

Capitalize on old-fashioned publicity stunts. No, you don't have to climb telephone poles or swallow goldfish to get attention, but you can make a name for yourself by having some fun at community events such as parades, cook-offs and arts-and-crafts fairs. Take part and let yourself and your employees go crazy with wacky T-shirts, fun slogans and more. Consider the landscaping company with a precision lawn-mowing team that does fancy footwork while marching in local parades.

Or how about the woman who manufactures authentic, three-alarm chili? She had a booth at a summer arts festival and wanted to create some additional attention for her product. She hired a volunteer fire department to show up with truck, ladders and firefighters decked out in full gear to spotlight her chili in a way no press release could.

155

Viewer's Choice

From Jack Trout and Al Ries

It's no surprise that marketing is not a battle of products—it's a battle of perceptions. Campbell's Soup is No. 1 in the United States, but not in the United Kingdom; Heinz Soup is No. 1 in the United Kingdom, but not in the United States. What that boils down to is the fact that packaging, design and image are just as important as delivering a quality product. And that's why marketing and advertising campaigns can make or break a product regardless of its quality. It's perception, not product.

When a man who owns an auto detailing business filmed a commercial in the pits of a major racetrack, the perception generated was "even the pros use this guy to keep their cars in mint condition." Even though he never said those drivers were his customers, the message was implied loud and clear.

156

Read All About It

From Betty Hoeffner

Publicity hounds need to know their media, so make an effort to read the magazines and newspapers or watch the broadcasts you are pitching to learn what kinds of stories they cover. Tailor your pitches to match their needs. For example, if a magazine or newspaper writes a regular column about financing a business, pitch them on how you raised the money to launch your company. Or for broadcast TV and radio shows that focus on health and fitness, send in a pitch about how your company's employees jog at lunch time. By gearing your pitches to each publication, you up your chances of getting coverage.

In addition, do this type of research for more than a week or two. Read several back issues, or watch a program for several months. Spend adequate time to get a true feel for what the medium is looking for. It also doesn't hurt to be a subscriber if you someday intend to appeal to the editor of a targeted magazine.

157

Hot Off The Press

From Rick Crandall

Any time your company or one of your clients is featured in a newspaper or magazine article, clip it out and have reprints made. Many publications offer reprint services for a reasonable fee. If they don't, cut out the article and make photocopies yourself. Most of the value of publicity comes long after a news article is published. You may get several calls when the article initially runs, but you'll get many more if you distribute reprints later. Adding press clips to your marketing materials makes your business look like big news.

That's what one catering company did after receiving an award for providing the best overall product for a gathering of more than 500 people. An industry association presented the company with this award and an article appeared in a major newspaper that covered the awards ceremony. From then on, a reprint of the article was included with every bid delivered for large-scale events.

158

Mind Over Matter

From Leann Anderson

There are times when you as a business owner may be interviewed by the press. This can be a wonderful opportunity to tell your company story or to send a specific message about your business. The key here is to make sure you know exactly what the reporter is looking for, and then be prepared to deliver a message that reflects positively on you. You can do this by knowing the parameters of the interview and thinking through what you want the public to know about you and your company.

When the owner of a sausage factory was interviewed about the relative safety of the sausage products available to most consumers, he spoke as an authority and answered the questions regarding safety within his industry. But because he was prepared, he also had made a mental list of the three key things he wanted to get across during the interview. He memorized that list and looked for ways to weave that information into his answers. He put his mind to work and addressed what mattered to him, as well as what mattered to the reporter.

159

Just The Facts, Ma'am

From Betty Hoeffner

In addition to knowing what key points you want to make during an interview, it's important to demonstrate that you know your stuff. Reporters deal with facts. So make sure you have some and that they're accurate and pertinent to the media you're targeting. Whatever facts you're pitching, make sure they tie into your business in some way. Before you call or fax a press release to a reporter, think of every question he or she might ask, and have answers prepared. Know what you want to say about your business and have all your facts on hand—dates, dollar figures, etc.

These types of figures were especially impressive when a small concrete contractor wanted his trade magazine and his local business journal to realize how experienced and proficient his employees were. He tallied all the yards of concrete he and his company had poured over the last 11 years and equated it with miles of highway. His comparison equaled a stretch of two-lane highway that would run from San Diego to Chicago. Now that got people's attention!

160

Mark The Date

From Betty Hoeffner

If you want to see your company's name in print, call the publications you're interested in and request an editorial calendar, which is a rundown of the major articles or themes a publication will cover throughout the year. This way, you'll know how and when to pitch the publication. Be sure to ask what the publication's lead time is—that's the number of months in advance that work begins on an issue. Note that many magazines work three to four months in advance, so don't wait until February to pitch a story for the February issue.

Let's say you wanted to promote the fact that your dairy delivers its products in a fleet of brand-new refrigerator trucks. You notice, however, that many of the calendars you checked indicate they have no interest in your mechanical achievements. They do, however, seem to like stories that show exceptional service or work ethics on the part of small companies. So you change your approach and focus on the fact the during the flood of 1992, yours was the only dairy in a 60-mile radius that stayed open and continued to produce milk, supplying area hospitals and schools for three days, 'round the clock.

161

Get In Their Faces

From Leslie Grossman

Use public relations to build your image. Whenever your company does something newsworthy—launching a new product, celebrating a grand opening, selling your one millionth product, adding a new service, winning a local business award—send a press release to local and national journalists. Get to know a few reporters and enlist the press in helping you to build public awareness of your business and its image. Image sells—to the media as well as to customers.

But keep in mind that what seems like a big deal to you might not be such a smashing event to the media. After all, reporters hear hundreds of pitches every year. So make sure your piece is truly newsworthy and presented in a way that's easy for the journalist to use. Don't cry wolf too often, or you'll never get noticed.

162

Talk The Talk

From Betty Hoeffner

What's one of the key secrets of getting through to reporters? Speak to your audience. If you're talking to a business reporter, use hard numbers—dollar growth, financial projections, initial investment, number of employees and the like. If you're talking to a tech editor, talk about how your company uses technology to improve sales. TV and photo editors understand visuals, so use phrases such as "picture this" to better communicate your idea. If you tailor your pitch to each specific reporter, you'll create a better rapport and improve your chances of seeing print.

A manufacturer of custom cabinets knows the magic of focusing on his audience. When speaking to a writer for a trade magazine, he emphasized the ease of installation and the quality of the materials. When talking to a writer for an interior design publication, he made a big deal about how beautiful and versatile the cabinets were, and he pointed out how many finishes and styles were available.

163

Get Hooked

From Betty Hoeffner

When appealing to a writer or reporter, always try to establish a news hook. Define something you do that nobody else does. Some business owners believe reporters should do stories on them because they serve good food or provide excellent service. That's like writing about a flight that didn't crash. That's not news. If you own a restaurant, you'd better be serving good food, and if you deliver a service, you should be striving for excellence. But if you're the only restaurant in town that hosts a cigar night or an annual three-legged race to combat hunger, that might be newsworthy.

Also keep in mind that reporters are always looking for good human-interest stories. If you have any employees or clients who stand out, share their stories with the press. For instance, if one of your employees is participating in a program designed to help the disabled become more self-sufficient, then have some background available on the history of the program, the struggle the employee has had to face, and the strides he's made.

164

Deadline News

From Betty Hoeffner

Be considerate of reporters' schedules. This is particularly important when you're dealing with newspapers and radio or TV news departments. If reporters are on deadline, the chances of tracking them down and delivering a lengthy pitch are slim to none. Before you start pitching, ask the reporter if he or she is on deadline. If the answer is yes, ask when it would be a good time to call back. If you insist on launching into your pitch when a harried reporter is on deadline, you risk damaging any relationship you might have built with that person. And you really run the risk of losing any chance you might have had of getting coverage.

Instead of pressing for the reporter's ear, be prepared to offer a 10-second synopsis of what you have to offer. For example, you might say "I'm calling to tell you about a new safety helmet designed especially for children under 4."

165

Photo Finish

From Rick Crandall

When pitching your business to publications, send some unusual photographs. Many times, media that cover service businesses are stuck with stale, sitting-at-the-desk photos that reporters and photo editors have seen thousands of times. Seek something photogenic about your business and strive for novel shots to distinguish yourself from the crowd.

One fellow decided to do something special for the ground-breaking ceremony for his ice cream shop. Instead of using the worn-out shovel image, he had giant ice cream scoops made and invited dignitaries to scoop some dirt for the camera. He spent the money to hire a professional photographer to take both color and black-and-white shots. He sent the black-and-white prints with press releases but noted that color photos were also available if needed. If you send photos, keep only a few color prints on hand and concentrate on the black-and-whites since most print media will prefer them.

166

Meet The Press

From Betty Hoeffner

Nearly every successful business owner knows the benefits of cultivating a trusting relationship with the press. Find common interests with reporters and be responsive to their requests. If a reporter needs information from you but isn't going to mention you or your company in the article, don't hem and haw. And don't try to play hardball by saying you'll turn over the information only if the reporter includes you in the story. Do the reporter and yourself a favor and get the information to him or her as soon as possible. The easier you can make a reporter's job, the more he or she will want to deal with you. And some day, the reporter just might find a way to squeeze your name into a story.

167

Perfect Pitch

From Betty Hoeffner

Know which publications and which reporters compete with each other. Don't pitch the same story to competing publications or stations; you may lose credibility with one or both. And don't simultaneously pitch two reporters at the same publication; reporters often compete with each other for stories. Pitching a whole roster of reporters at media outlets where reporters don't compete can backfire, too. The shotgun approach rarely produces results.

So if you're serious about wanting some reputable coverage of the new diagnostic equipment in your international auto repair shop, contact the reporter at the publication or station you find most reliable, and give him an exclusive. Let him know you've followed his career and respect his approach. Then give him ample information and pitch it in a way that really says "Here's something new and powerful."

168

Referral Service

From Betty Hoeffner

You should always attempt to target a single reporter at any media outlet with your story idea. But knowing the right reporter to contact isn't easy. The titles you read in newspaper and magazine mastheads don't always give a good indication of what each editor or writer covers; the same goes for the closing credits on TV shows. If you're not sure who to call, pick a name and launch into an abbreviated pitch by asking who the best reporter would be to cover that type of story. If one reporter turns down your idea, don't close the book on that publication or broadcast station. Ask if anyone else at the media outlet would be interested.

If necessary, use another approach or give a backup pitch. If your initial spin doesn't get anyone's attention, move on to a second angle that might. But don't start rattling off a litany of ideas. Remember, you should have done your homework and know something about the reporter or media source you've contacted.

169

Publicity Pays

From Danielle Kennedy

Doing good deeds in the community, introducing new products, being an expert in your field—these are all things that will help your business, but if the public doesn't hear about your accomplishments, your efforts won't have the same impact. To get the word out, hire a public relations consultant. If you aren't too creative, ask the experts to give you the identification you need to make an impact in the marketplace.

And remember, budgeting for PR help can be just as legitimate an expense as buying an ad in the newspaper. The coverage you get won't cost you a thing, so the expense of hiring a pro can take the place of buying ads. Plus, the "third party" endorsement value that comes from an article or a piece on the evening news can have value way beyond a dollar figure.

170

Thanksgiving

From Betty Hoeffner

When a reporter does a story on your company, it's a good idea to thank him or her with a phone call or card. You don't need to go overboard and send lavish gifts; in fact, many reporters cannot accept gifts from the people they interview. However, staying in touch following a write-up is a good way to build a relationship with that reporter and improve the possibility of a second or even third story.

A couple who run a mobile computer consulting service found themselves the subject of a feature story on businesses that come to you. Because of the coverage they got, their business volume skyrocketed, so to thank the reporter, they created a personalized "floppy coupon." It was a simple disk that had a clever "thank you" message and an offer of a free hour of computer assistance for the reporter or one of his colleagues.

171

Star Power

From Jerry Fisher

Elvis' former hair stylist (and astrologer) markets a book of grooming tips for staying youthful-looking—just as he managed to keep The King looking well-coiffed during his heyday. So if you cut the hair, clean the clothes, fix the plumbing or zap the termites of somebody well-known in your community, see if you can use his or her name—within reason—to promote your enterprise. In Tinseltown, marketers are constantly touting the fact that their clients include TV and movie stars. And, surprisingly, it works! Many customers think that if you're good enough for someone rich and famous, you must be good enough for them.

To bring this notion closer to home, take a look at the football team from a small university that won the national championship. A local manufacturer of canvas bags supplied the entire team with travel luggage and took lots of video of how the bags were manhandled over the season. This seemed to be a popular testimonial to how well the luggage was made, plus it was a fun way to showcase the hometown winners.

172

PR 911

From Betty Hoeffner

If you have a good story, but reporters continually turn you down, it may be because of the way you communicate with them or the way your press releases are written. After all, what you find most interesting about your company might not be what appeals to outsiders. Ask friends and employees to review your press releases and listen to your story pitch and then ask them for their honest input and questions. You may find a new way to present your story that will make it more appealing to reporters.

A case in point: A vegetable farmer developed an organic fertilizer that causes vegetables to grow 50 percent more than most vegetables. While the farmer was taken with the organic nature of his product, his friends and customers couldn't stop talking about the giant eggplants that were so large that they looked like purple watermelons.

173

Drop The 'Tude

From Betty Hoeffner

I f there is one golden piece of advice to heed regarding getting publicity for your product or service, it would be this: Treat the media with respect. Be friendly and helpful to all media representatives, whether they're calling you for information or you're calling them to pitch a story. When you make a pitch, you might think you're going to get patched directly through to the editor-in-chief, but, more likely, you're going to be speaking with an assistant or lower-level editor. Whatever you do, don't be snobbishly presumptuous, insisting that you'll only speak with someone "important." Reporters are constantly jumping from one publication to another; the cub reporter you snub today could be the editor of a national publication tomorrow.

Chapter 15

Network News

174

Netiquette

From Leslie Grossman

Network—and always communicate your image. In fact, try becoming active in professional and community associations and groups. Whenever you introduce yourself, introduce your business as well. Use your positioning statement to give people a brief overall view of what your business does. This doesn't apply only to formal networking occasions; you can reinforce your business's reputation by using your positioning statement wherever you go.

One woman who runs a private day-care facility knows the value of networking. She also believes in giving back to society through some form of community service. So when she volunteered to help build a battered children's shelter, it was easy for her to offer a few hours of free day care to the children of parents who were doing the physical labor needed to get the shelter up and going.

175

A Little Help From Your Friends

From Danielle Kennedy

ooking for leads? Why not form your own local business network? Make it a point to know local noncompeting businesses. Invite them to attend networking meetings and make sure to have some sort of agenda of topics that affect all of you: marketing ideas that work, zoning laws, local consumer demographics, etc. A well-known computer entrepreneur opened her business in a town where she was unknown, but that changed when she got together with other business owners every quarter to share leads and marketing ideas. Today, she owns a multimillion-dollar company.

Follow suit. Take a look at your own situation and develop a list of key businesses you'd like to know more about or share information with. Be the first to extend an invitation to get together and swap ideas, and have in mind some notion for how the group can continue to function.

176

What's In A Name?

From Martin R. Baird

If you're looking for referrals, who better to tap than your existing customers? Most likely, they know other people who share similar interests, needs and buying power. Generating referrals from current customers is one of the best ways to market your business. Just do a thorough job of explaining exactly what kind of referrals you're looking for and how they can help. Be sure, too, that you thank them, assure them of their privacy if that is a concern, and offer a coupon or small gift to show your appreciation.

And remember, your customers are not the only ones to tap for referrals. Don't forget to query your vendors (they're likely to have many contacts). The next time you place an order or use a vendor's services, ask him or her to take a moment for a cup of coffee with you. Then plant the referral seed in his or her mind and watch it grow.

177

Meet Market

From Danielle Kennedy

In business, you can't do it alone; sometimes your best leads will come from people who aren't even in your industry. Don't make the mistake of thinking that the only people who can help build your business are ones who are directly related to your field. Other professionals can be a great source for leads or might be able to help your business when you're considering expanding into new markets, breaking ground on a new location or seeking financing. Make it a point to meet the key people in town who can help grow your business. This could mean a prominent attorney, banker, realtor or accountant. Don't wait for the next chamber of commerce meeting to introduce yourself.

The owner of a company that created "earth grain pastas with the heavenly taste" decided the best way to meet influential people was through his product. He sent a small sample of one of his pastas to each of the people on his list and included a request for a few minutes of their time. Almost every person remembered his unique "greeting" and made time to get acquainted.

178

Be All That You Can Be

From Nancy Michaels

People like to do business with individuals they perceive as confident and capable, not to mention those who have excellent reputations. Consequently, it's worth making an effort to maintain that image. You might think that as an entrepreneur you should be slaving away in the office 24 hours a day, but making appearances on the social scene can do just as much for your business as making cold calls from the office. Getting to know the right people—professionals and other business owners—can provide you with a network of leads and contacts.

The key thing to remember, however, is why you're there in the first place. Don't get caught up in too much socializing on one end of the spectrum, or too much selling on the other. Find a blend. Have something original and memorable to say about your business so that when you meet people, they'll have a fighting chance of remembering who you are. Someone who says "I'm an interior designer who specializes in bringing the outside in" certainly gives you a mental image to attach to a name.

179

Lead The Way

From Danielle Kennedy

When it comes to seeking out leads, don't be shy. Host a leads breakfast and invite local entrepreneurs who aren't direct competitors. You may get more than you bargained for—in addition to adding potential customers to your list, you might also find suppliers, vendors and members of other professions whose services you may need. Invite a lawyer, politician or security expert to speak to the group about a topic that's of interest to everyone involved.

This step goes beyond simply forming a networking group. It implies a bit more structure and a more determined approach. By adding the element of an informative talk on a topic of interest to the business community, it also allows you to assume a position of responsibility and visibility. You're doing something for the rest of the group and providing a service of sorts. People warm up quickly to the generosity of others.

180

Leisure World Leads

From Rick Crandall

Network in unique places. Don't rule out traffic school, bowling leagues and other nonbusiness events as chances to share your story. The more hobbies and group activities you participate in, the more opportunities you'll have to spread the word about your business. Leisure activities such as softball leagues, golf lessons and aerobics classes provide a natural setting for networking and encourage relationship-building more often than the stiff introductions typical of most formal networking events. Leads will come your way from these avenues without your having to do the hard sell.

181

Neighborhood Watch

From Danielle Kennedy

Don't forget to network with people you know. We tend to think networking is about constantly meeting new people; we forget about neighbors and friends as sources of leads. Always make it a point to talk up business with acquaintances and tell them about new products, new projects and new directions. In conversation, don't be afraid to directly ask friends and neighbors for leads.

A woman who carries a line of custom clothing that she sells from her home branched out to a new market because of networking with a friend. Her friend had recently undergone a mastectomy and said she was having trouble finding stylish, sporty clothes to fit. The entrepreneur realized then and there that a market existed for these types of garments, and she found many friends and neighbors willing to share names and leads with her as soon as she told them about her new line.

182

Refer Madness

From Nancy Michaels

Business-to-business operators should always provide clients with referrals. If you're doing business with a company, you ought to be referring people to them. People always appreciate new leads, and giving referrals conveys your value to customers in a tangible way. Clients will also be likely to return the favor not only by buying from you in the future, but also by sending some referrals your way. That means you win in more ways than one.

The important thing here is to remember to have your antennae up. Be a good listener and a keen observer. One owner of a camera shop always makes a point to ask his customers a question or two that can help him remember them the next time they come in. By doing this, he not only improves his relationship with clients and his ability to serve them, but he uses his mental notes to make connections that can help his customers' businesses thrive. For instance, when a woman came in who needed a dozen photos of antique settees developed, he saw instantly that his friend in the upholstery business might be of help to her. He mentally connected the dots.

Chapter 16

Find
Your Focus

183

Stay On The Straight And Narrow

From Jack Trout

There is no magic formula for successful marketing, but there is one guiding principle—stay focused. Great brands stay focused on their concepts. When a brand *loses its focus*, bad things happen. That doesn't mean you can't expand at all; just don't stray from your core business or the reason why customers came to you in the first place.

Consider, for example, a firm that specializes in generating medical reports quickly and accurately. Its founders built a large medical clientele consisting of clinics and individuals based on a 24-hour turnaround time in generating reports. When they started adding services for insurance agents, financial planners and so on, they weakened their original position and started losing clients because their service suffered. Eventually, they went back to making their "main thing" their "main thing."

184

Don't Go Changing

From Jay Conrad Levinson

Restraint is your ally when it comes to marketing. Resist your natural inclination to change things. Don't jump from a print ad in a magazine one month to a radio spot the next month, then to distributing fliers in the neighborhood. Altering the message in your ads is another no-no. Customers need to know they can lean on you, and if you're constantly changing your message, your identity and your media, you'll be too elusive for most people.

While there is some debate about the aesthetic value of using billboard advertising, a couple who own a music store spent an entire year's worth of their marketing budget working with an agency to generate six colossal billboard advertisements. The ads, which each featured a magnificent photo of an instrument, were placed selectively along routes that were traveled by people who fit their ideal demographic profile. People began to talk about the images and anticipated when the next one would appear. The message and the medium were constant, and their profits were, too.

185

Don't Mess With Success

From Jack Trout

The most powerful brands don't change. Some shooting-star brands come and go, like People's Express. It was a great concept—small airline, small prices. It took off like a rocket. Then it changed. And now it's gone.

If you're tempted to make some changes in your business, take time to consider all the pluses and minuses before you even glance in another direction. When a successful sporting goods store decided to open a training/diagnostic center next door, it seemed like a good idea on the surface. But because it took so much time, money and effort to get it up and going, the charm, personal attention and quality merchandising that made the store a hit in the first place suffered greatly. Long after a swing is video-taped or a stance is analyzed, people will still just want to buy great equipment from people who know their products.

186

Give And Ye Shall Receive

From Jack Trout and Al Ries

You have to give up something to get something. Emery Air Freight, once the leader in air-freight shipping, offered rush service, economy service and small and large package delivery. Federal Express sacrificed, focused on delivering small packages overnight—and put Emery out of business. You need to focus on one core component or one market segment, especially when you're just starting out. Developing a single product or service is much easier and far less costly than trying to offer a whole product line and a host of services. Keep it simple.

187

Patience, Please

From Jay Conrad Levinson

The foremost personality characteristic of the successful guerrilla is patience. If you are patient, you can practice commitment, treat marketing as an investment and be consistent. But if you're impatient and expect things to happen fast, you'll fall into the trap of changing directions, media and your messages in hopes of finding a quick fix. Remember that marketing is a long-term project. Patient people do not expect miracles—just results.

That lesson held true for one man who runs an accounting firm. He started out offering services and advice primarily to small businesses. While he was tempted along the way to broaden his clientele, he decided his niche might just be the ever-growing pool of small and home-based businesses that were popping up all over the community. He stayed true to his mission of giving big results to small business.

Chapter **17**

Win The
Goodwill
Games

188

Get Involved

From Danielle Kennedy

Marketing doesn't always revolve around advertising campaigns and sales pitches. There are some types of activities that fall into the "plant the seeds now, and reap the harvest later" category. Community involvement is a great example of this kind of activity because you frequently won't see results right away. The benefits are more long-term.

Your options here are endless: Help organize a 10K run for the American Diabetes Association or put together a food drive for the homeless. Giving back to your community lets you do good and, at the same time, drums up business.

189

The Good Guys

From Edith Weiner

Spiritual fulfillment is becoming big business. People are looking to products and services that bolster their sense of well-being and self-esteem; they're also expecting companies to exhibit integrity and social responsibility. These days, more marketing is based on morality than on cut-and-dried profit-seeking. Performing good deeds is good news for your fellow citizens, but you can make it great news for your business, too. Make sure you let your customers know about your company's good deeds, or your efforts won't impact your business.

For example, if your company is making a concerted effort to use biodegradable products and recycle everything from paper to motor oil, make a big deal about your conscientious practices. Include factoids about what you're doing in your newsletter, your invoices or even on your voice-mail greetings.

190

Take Responsibility

From Carol Coletta

Make social responsibility an integral part of your marketing mix. More than 60 percent of American adults say they will switch retail stores based on the store's involvement in a good cause if price and quality are equal. And 80 percent say they think a company involved in its community is more likely to be concerned about satisfying customers. But don't expect social responsibility to compensate for not being competitive on product, price and service. It can't and it won't.

What it will do, however, is persuade that fence sitter to come on over and do business with you. It can be the one thing that helps make a reluctant customer a committed one. So build "doing good" into your marketing mix the same way you build in a direct-mail piece. You should include a social responsibility schedule and budget in your marketing plan.

191

Goodwill Works

From Michel Roux

Do well by doing good—give back to the community whenever possible. We have an obligation to help people in our community who are less fortunate than we are. A percentage of the profits you make comes from the community, and you should reinvest in it. Find ways to invest that will not only benefit the community but also your business. For instance, investing in economic revitalization projects that will spur business growth creates a win-win situation.

Or on a smaller scale, set aside one day a month as your "nonprofit day"—literally! Publicly commit to giving the profits you make one day a month to a community project, and make a big deal about it. Have a banner made or place an ad in your local paper reminding people that their purchases that day will help support something that will enhance their community.

192

Give And Take

From Carol Coletta

Don't forget that there is a distinction between socially responsible marketing and philanthropy. Philanthropy benefits a charity with no expectation of return to the donor. Social responsibility marketing initiatives (SRMIs) should be true win-win situations—the community wins, and so does your business. Don't expect immediate monetary gains from your SRMI; the benefits are usually of a different nature—added publicity, increased brand awareness, introduction of your product to new markets and so on.

One man who opened a new, high-tech, no-touch car wash took this notion to heart. He offered his facility to the boys and girls club in his community for a car wash fund-raiser. The drive-thru wash was his donation, and the kids then vacuumed and dried the cars for $5. He not only was able to provide a means of generating dollars for the club, but introduced hundreds of people to his facility in a socially responsible way.

193

Do The Right Thing

From Michel Roux

Be a responsible marketer. It's important to make sure what you're putting in the box or bottle is really what you say you're selling, not something else. It's up to you to implement quality control measures to ensure that your products are top-notch and safe. Being a responsible marketer often means going beyond quality control issues and considering ethical or moral obligations. For instance, in the spirits industry, this means making sure you're encouraging people to drink responsibly.

Likewise, if you're in a business where there is a potentially harmful byproduct, take steps to ensure quality or safety. Renting in-line skates without insisting that customers wear helmets and pads is not an example of doing the right thing.

194

Make It Count

From Carol Coletta

If you're going to engage in socially responsible marketing, pick a cause that's relevant to your customers. American Express and restaurant merchants team up to fight hunger. Builders Square sponsors Safe and Secure Month to encourage people to keep their homes safe. The Texas book chain Half Price Books promotes literacy. To be successful, the cause must be one that matters, deeply, to your core customers.

If you can't settle on a particular cause that has broad customer appeal, then look to an age-appropriate activity (you don't want to host a wine-tasting if your target market is families) or community project (painting houses for people who are disabled) that's popular across the board. Let's say you own a bicycle shop. In that case, spearheading a fund-raiser to help construct a bike trail along a river would probably be something your customers would like.

195

Pass The Word

From Carol Coletta

Too often, employees are the last to know about promotions. That's a fatal mistake with SRMIs. Employees must be able to communicate to customers the real level of caring involved in these campaigns. And, just like customers, employees will feel stronger ties to your company if they are involved in team projects like SRMIs. Putting employees directly in touch with customers who are active in charitable promotions gives your staff a better understanding of who your customers are.

One hardware store that has great employee involvement in every one of its promotions makes sure employees know well in advance what the SRMI will be. In fact, they are consulted a month ahead of time and asked for suggestions about what worthy causes the business should focus on. Then they're trained and rewarded with special T-shirts and a modest gift certificate to a local restaurant to show the owner's appreciation.

196

Take It Easy

From Carol Coletta

Creating an SRMI shouldn't require you to add additional staff or engage in activities you know nothing about. The recipe for success is simple: Instead of making it a hardship, do what you do best. Home Depot employees build low-cost homes for Habitat for Humanity. Avon sales representatives distribute breast cancer awareness literature to customers. Do what makes sense for your line of business, your skills and your culture.

A great example comes from a small company that installs and repairs heating and air-conditioning systems. Once in the spring and once in the fall, employees volunteer to check the appropriate systems for people who are disabled or simply incapable of handling these jobs themselves.

197

Do Your Part

From Marlene Rossman

There's value in becoming involved in the community where your target market lives. You can support grass-roots activities by participating on a companywide basis. Sponsor a Little League team or a children's night at the YMCA, and you'll earn recognition as a good citizen, plus you'll probably meet potential customers in the process.

Multicultural communities appreciate businesses that support the neighborhood. The key to doing this effectively is to make every effort to really learn about the neighborhood and the activities that take place there.

For instance, a roofing company located in a part of a community that has a strong ethnic identity realized that traditional activities for young people weren't what was popular in its neighborhood. What was hot? Boxing. So the roofing company bought gloves, helmets and robes for the kids who were committed, responsible participants. The payoff came in a mutual respect that was created for the equipment and people involved.

198

Put Your Customers To Work

From Carol Coletta

The best SRMIs are not promotions where you do something good and then tell your customers about it; they involve customers. Getting customers in on the act makes them feel good about doing good and strengthens their ties to your company. For example: Department store chain Carson Pirie Scott collected worn coats from customers for needy women and rewarded donors with a discount on new coats. They made it easy for customers to do good. Once your campaign or project is completed, be sure to acknowledge what your customers did. Give them a public pat on the back.

199

Get Creative

From Danielle Kennedy

To really make a splash in community involvement, you need to be just as creative as you are in your business. Every year, thousands of companies go the usual charity route—sponsoring races and contributing to food drives. But if you sponsor offbeat, memorable events, you'll make a real name for your company. In addition to more traditional events, try unusual ideas like renting a movie theater for a day and inviting kids to a free viewing. Do this toward the end of the summer, before school starts, about the time parents are ready to go nuts.

Or maybe you happen to own a pet store. Why not organize a pet health and beauty fair? You could coordinate with area veterinarians and animal groomers for a day of no-cost or low-cost checkups and perk-ups for small animals. For a small investment, a great deal of goodwill and positive publicity could result.

No Money Required

From Carol Coletta

You may think that your business is too small and cash-strapped to be able to come to the aid of a charitable organization. But you should recognize that money is probably the least valuable of your resources. Donating time, equipment and manpower are often more effective than dumping cash into a charity. In fact, corporate giving represents less than 5 percent of the total philanthropy in America.

To illustrate the real power and value behind giving your time and talent, check out this story. When a small town was in danger of losing its historic train depot, numerous citizens rallied and committed to restoring the building to its original beauty. The owner of a nearby bagel and coffee shop not only supplied free goodies to the volunteers, but his employees showed up for the early shift and worked a collective total of 65 hours.

201

And The Winner Is . . .

From Rick Crandall

I f you want publicity, give an award to a member of your community. A landscaper could present awards for the best lawns in the neighborhood; an environmental consultant could present an award for the most environmentally sound business. For more publicity, make it an annual competition where locals enter to win. For example, a caterer might host a cook-off for the best holiday cookie recipe. The winner would not only receive a prize, but the recipe would be used in your holiday catering. You win all the way around—publicity, goodwill and a stronger link to the community and potential customers.

Don't Overdo It

From Carol Coletta

The visibility that comes with an SRMI will likely generate requests for help from other charities. And if your SRMI had positive results for your business, you may be tempted to jump on other offers to do similar projects. Hey, if one project produced good results, then two or three projects should be even better, right? Wrong! It's far better to do one project well, with impact, than to scatter your resources across a half dozen projects.

A fitness center saw the wisdom of this philosophy when it decided to sponsor an annual challenge weekend. Teams of volunteers participated in fitness contests, and every team had to line up contributions and sponsors in advance. The winning team received prizes and recognition while the money collected went to charity; the fitness center picked up all the expenses associated with holding the event. Participation increased, and the event's visibility grew year after year. The center's management was frequently asked to sponsor other events, but they knew the value in being the key player in their weekend activity. So take a lesson from them, and be prepared to say no when too many requests are made of you.

203

I Feel Good!

From Carol Coletta

When it comes to giving back to your community, whatever you decide to do, do it with feeling. After all, that's what this is all about—feeling good and making a difference in your community and your business. If your efforts are solely for the sake of improving your bottom line, you won't get the full personal benefits that come with giving back. And feeling good for doing good is something that will never go out of style.

An advertising agency CEO found this to be true when she decided to be one of the lead sponsors for an athletic event involving disabled children. At first she committed to it only because it got great press and made her company look good. But the second year, she decided to be a volunteer and work the event. She was never so moved or so enthusiastic about anything in her life, and that genuine passion couldn't be faked. Thanks to a little goodwill, her company got loads of good press and good feelings from the participation.

Chapter 18

Go The
Extra Mile

204

Do Unto Others

From Guy Kawasaki

Don't ask your customers to do what you wouldn't do. For instance, would you wait an hour for tech support? Would you send a letter to get your statement adjusted? Neither would your customers. Make it easy for them to do business with you or they'll do business somewhere else.

This philosophy hit home with the owner of a large furniture store who had to wait an entire day for the delivery of his new computer system at his home. He asked for an approximate time of delivery, but all he got was "Sometime on the 12th." He was steaming by the time it arrived, and, as a result, he vowed to never make his customers wait at home for more than a two-hour period. He even promises that his delivery people will call when they're within a half hour of arrival.

205

R-E-S-P-E-C-T

From Maxwell Sroge

It seems like a no-brainer to remind yourself to treat people with respect. This goes back to the idea of realizing nothing is more valuable than your customers. All your customers deserve respect, not just your biggest ones. You never know—that guy who always buys your least expensive item could be your biggest customer tomorrow. So treat them right.

When one fellow walked into a storefront for a company that makes all sorts of shipping containers, all he wanted was a heavy-duty cardboard box that had hand slits on the sides for easy carrying. Even though the owner of the shop was busy, he stopped to help the customer find exactly the right size box to meet his needs. The customer was so pleased with the personal, pleasant attention he received that he called the next day and asked the owner to meet with him about handling all the shipping boxes for the light fixtures manufactured by his company.

206

Honesty Is The Best Policy

From Peter Connolly

The foundation of any successful relationship is trust. It provides security, credibility and reliability. Some business owners will promise a prospect the sun and the moon to make the sale, knowing full well they can't deliver. While they may make that sale, they'll probably never see that customer again. Don't make any promises you can't keep. If you tell a customer the product he or she ordered will be delivered on a certain date, make darn sure it arrives on that precise day. When you sign a contract to incorporate components A, B and C into a project, you'd better include those three items. Promote honesty with your workers and customers, and in return, you'll get loyalty.

207

Three-In-One

From Edith Weiner

In the past, entertainment, education and information were three separate businesses, and you didn't have to be in any one of them to sell your product or service. Increasingly, however, these are becoming a single business, and you have to be in that business to be successful. Whatever you sell must have a strong knowledge component, must educate your customers, and certainly must be entertaining. This goes for everything from toys to tech products.

To make sure their facility meets the "EEI" formula, the owners of a large Laundromat take extra steps to cater to their customers. Because the bulk of their users are college students, they provide televisions in several corners of the building, ample tables and chairs, and even extra electrical outlets near the tables so that laptop computers can be plugged in.

Exceed The Need

From Philip Nulman

Everybody talks about customer satisfaction, but you need to go way beyond that. Don't just satisfy customers—delight them in ways they didn't expect. Try providing free delivery, 24-hour customer service, and incentives. Reinforce your commitment to them at all times. Not sure how to go the extra mile? Simply ask your customers what additional services they would most appreciate. Chances are, they'll be more than happy to tell you.

An auto dealer tried this and really applied what he learned. He asked many of his customers what would delight them about doing business with his dealership. They gave him a long list of ideas. Two weeks later, he was implementing many of their suggestions, including making sure the customer's car was washed and vacuumed after it was serviced, providing shuttle or loaner cars when customers needed rides, and staying within 30 minutes of the quoted finish time or letting them know as soon as possible if repairs would take longer.

209

Open For Business

From Edith Weiner

You may think that as an entrepreneur, you get to set your own hours, but successful business owners know that their customers are the ones who determine when, where and how they work. Be ready to be where your customers want you, when your customers want you, with what your customers want. Just-in-time marketing is critical as people become spoiled by 24-hour, seven-days-a-week customized products and services. If you aren't available when customers call, it's too easy for them to take their business elsewhere.

Now you might be saying "Yes, but no one can be available 24 hours a day." True, but you can have a voice-mail system that gives more than just the typical "leave a message" information. Everything from customized mailboxes to personalized extensions are available. Or consider using a "fax on demand" feature that allows a caller to request anything from a current catalog to this year's price list, simply by pushing a button or two.

210

100 Ways To Win Customers

From Martin R. Baird

When faced with the purchase of big-ticket items, and even some low-priced goods, consumers can feel fearful that they won't like the product, that it will break or that it just won't meet their expectations. The same goes for services. Want to make it easier for consumers to buy from you? Offer a 100 percent guarantee. If you eliminate the risk, consumers will feel much more comfortable about purchasing your product or service. Emphasize the fact that you offer a guarantee—and be sure to honor your promise with a hassle-free return policy.

The owners of a new lawn-care service offer a 100 percent guarantee that they can rid your lawn of crab grass or "die tryin'." They've tested their techniques again and again, and found that if they add a particular step to the process, it never fails to work. They feel they're different from their competition and want to guarantee that difference. Occasionally, that means a return trip or two, but their follow-up is impeccable and their commitment to quality service always wins over new prospects.

211

Cuckoo For Custom-Made

From Watts Wacker

Today, everyone has overwhelming access to unbelievable levels of products and services. Some 65 million people have already been on TV shows or news programs, for instance. And even the least-affluent households in America have things like color televisions, telephones, multiple rooms and private bathrooms. So one of the issues that will be of great concern in the future will be scarcity. What is scarce? Products designed specifically for you. Manufacturing will become a service business. Even Levi's are now custom-made.

If you want your business to stand apart from the rest, you've got to customize your product and service as much as possible. Whether it's burgers or ski boots that you sell, hair cuts or health care that you give, do it with all the personalization that's reasonable. Let your database be your anchor for never forgetting who likes what, and how they like it.

212

Got Time?

From Jay Conrad Levinson

People no longer believe that old axiom "Time is money." They know time is much more valuable than money, so they expect and demand convenience. You've got to knock yourself out making it easy for people to buy what you're selling. Make sure your hours of operation and availability mesh with the needs of your customers. And never waste your customers' time.

A great example of not wasting clients' time comes from an interior decorating firm that has only four employees. Amazingly, it does more business than companies with three times as many employees. Why? Instead of making customers come to the shop and pore through literally hundreds of books, employees interview clients ahead of time and fill out a profile sheet to help them pull samples that might appeal to the customer. Then, when clients come in, they have a table set up and a sample bin prepared. They even have several little metal luggage carriers, the kind that flight attendants use, for their clients to borrow. They just load up the sample books, bag the small stuff and strap them onto the carrier. Clients love this special treatment.

213

Don't Forget Those Little Extras

From Jerry Fisher

Just plain thank-you notes may be a bit old hat, so find creative ways to thank your customers. Sending a small token of your appreciation gives customers that personal touch that keeps them coming back for more. Find a small gift that relates to your business that will make customers think of you every time they see it. A precious-metals investment firm might, for example, offer investors a free, classy little gold Canadian maple leaf with accompanying 12-karat gold chain in return for having invested in 20 1-ounce gold maple leaves through them.

Or on a smaller scale, if you own a shoe store, then supply your customers with a shoe-shine sponge or scuff mitt with your store name on it. Encourage them to put one in their glove compartments, have one in their desk drawers and keep one at home. They'll get in the habit of using them and want to keep up the practice. It will be a natural step for them to come back to you for their next pair of shoes.

214

Surprise And Delight

From Leann Anderson

When going the extra mile to serve your customers, you don't necessarily have to spend a lot of time and money to make a great impression. Frequently, it's when people are surprised and delighted that they are most appreciative of you and your business.

The owners of one floral company take this philosophy to heart: They surprise a customer with flowers for no reason other than that the customer is loyal and has been with them for a long time. They also deliver a thank-you bouquet one year after a new customer first used their services. Word gets around and everyone loves to be surprised with a thoughtful gift when least expected.

Chapter 19

It's A
Free-For-All

215

The Gift Of Giving

From Martin R. Baird

Nearly every type of business—whether you sell a product or a service—can benefit from offering gift certificates. They're an easy, low-cost way to generate immediate revenue you can put to use until they're cashed in. And it's a great way to introduce new customers to your business. If people receive gift certificates to your company, chances are they'll stop in to redeem them even if they've never heard of your company before. Always ask your customers if they'd like to purchase gift certificates and offer them in several denominations.

This tip is especially useful for businesses that offer a wide selection of products, like a bookstore or music shop, where literally thousands of titles and topics are available. So if your business has an abundance of choices associated with it, encourage the use of gift certificates. Then be sure to show your appreciation by packaging the certificate in a fancy container with a classy look to it. Some people feel let down when all they have to present as a gift is an envelope. Think creatively and make your certificate cry out for attention!

216

Offer Appetizers

From Jerry Fisher

Never underestimate the benefits of whetting the prospect's appetite for more by offering a free trial period for your service. Your free offer should give prospects a taste of what you can do for them and it should definitely leave them wanting more. For example, a national video dating service entices prospects into its centers by inviting them to become members for a day. Once there, the prospects view sample videos of prospective dates in their age groups, the way they would as full-fledged members—but without being privy to names or addresses. This whets prospects' appetites for more, which, of course, they can only get by becoming bona fide members.

217

Go On Trial

From Martin R. Baird

Bigger isn't always better. A tiny trial size or sample of your product can produce big results. And a taste of your service can lead to bigger things. If you can get someone to try your product or service, chances are he or she will buy it later. And the best way to get someone to try something is to give it away for free. Have employees pass out product samples in front of your business; if you provide a service, you can offer, for example, one free week out of a four-week trial period.

A trio of graduate students who were studying horticulture decided to start a "rehab" service for sick plants at offices and homes. They guaranteed they could perk up almost any ailing flora. To prove their point, they offered a week of free plant care with the purchase of two weeks of service. Their clients saw a big difference after three weeks and most of them were sold for the long haul.

218

Whose Side Are You On?

From Nancy Michaels

Customers love the word "free." And even though giving away freebies may cost you in the short term, giving something away for free can boost profits in the long run. It's good for clients to know you're not charging them for everything you do. It promotes goodwill and makes customers feel like you're on their side. Offer a free service or a discount coupon as a reward for continued business.

For example, the owner of a travel agency trains her employees to think about "little extras." The agency's standard wrap-up when clients come in for service is to have them leave with something more than they came in with. Maybe it's only little chocolates in the shape of a cruise ship. Or maybe they leave with inflatable travel pillows for those long flights across the Pacific. Things like free passport photos, luggage tags and maps are all part of the agency's "little extras" mentality. As a result, it has lots of repeat business and happy customers.

219

Great Giveaways

From Dan Peña

If you're sure of yourself and your work's as good as you think it is, you end up getting paid many times for a marketing effort that was free in the first place. Whether you provide a service or sell a product, you can find a way to give something away for free. Make sure your giveaway is a small sample or taste of your product or a glimpse of what you can do for customers. The trick is to get the free item or trial service to entice prospects to come back for more. So don't make your giveaway a throwaway.

You might even want to take a hint from one hair salon owner. Whenever a client has a concern or asks about a new way to deal with a hair problem, she makes a note on a file card right in front of them. In this way, she demonstrates she's really listening. Then, before the client comes in again, she researches the issue and finds a product or two to try before actually giving the client a sample to test before he or she purchases anything. She finds a solution most of the time, but even when the problem can't be fixed, the owner earns points for trying so hard.

220

It's On The House

From Jerry Fisher

A tried and true method you may want to consider is to offer something "on the house." You may think it's going to negatively impact your bottom line if you dole out giveaways to prospective customers. Sure, it can impact your bottom line, but usually it will be in a positive way. A privately run airport parking lot, for example, could send mailers to frequent fliers and include three free parking passes, each good for 24 hours of free parking per visit. The lure of parking "on the house" draws prospects in so they can appreciate firsthand just how convenient, safe and roomy the lot is—and how affordable it is to park there regularly.

221

Freebies! Freebies! Freebies!

From Martin R. Baird

You may already have a roster of customers who buy from you on a regular basis, but how do you get them to buy more from you? It's simple—create incentives. Offer customers free merchandise or services after they buy a certain amount to get them in the habit of purchasing again and again. Try handing out punch cards to customers and punching them each time they make purchases; after 10 purchases, give them a freebie. Or tell customers that if they buy $50 worth of merchandise, they get 5 percent off; $75, they get 10 percent off; or $100, they get 15 percent off. These tactics might not bring in more customers, but they definitely make customers spend more.

Take, for instance, the hosiery and lingerie shop that has a punch card for hosiery purchases. Twenty pairs of hose gets you a free cosmetic or travel bag. If you're in the checkout line and have purchased only 18 pairs, wouldn't you go ahead and buy the extra two pairs just to get the bag on this trip to the store instead of on your next visit?

Handout Helper

From Jerry Fisher

Put something in prospects' hands. This will give you a leg up on getting them to place an order. This doesn't mean you have to give out free product samples. Your handout can be something that relates to your company. For example, an inner-city mission for the homeless might solicit donations by mailing prospective donors a set of unique cardboard tokens dubbed "Mission—Spare Change." When a homeless person comes up to you asking for spare change, give him or her one of these tokens good for a hot meal at the mission. You can do a good deed without wondering if your handout is going for drugs or alcohol. The donor buys into this idea by sending a donation to the mission.

Or you can follow the lead of a man who owns a sporting goods store that caters primarily to people who like to hunt and fish. He never lets a customer leave his store without giving him or her a small card with a painting of a game fish or bird on it. The paintings are reproductions of classic originals, and customers can find information about the featured species on the back. The laminated cards have become collectibles.

Chapter 20

Get 'Em In
On The Act

223

Speak The Same Language

From Leslie Grossman

You cannot build an image alone, so be sure to include your team in your image marketing plan. Make sure every employee—from the receptionist to the driver to the customer service rep—knows your positioning statement and understands how to communicate the business's position to your target audience. If employees don't know what your company's position is, they'll give customers mixed messages, which dilutes the impact of your marketing efforts.

A small company that processes film has three locations. Its goal is to have photos ready for customers in about one hour. The owner has shared his philosophy with his employees and has empowered them to make a decision on the spot if for some reason a customer is unhappy or disappointed with the service or work. Time and again, a potentially lost customer has been retained and won over because an employee instantly apologized for whatever happened (even if it was unavoidable) and gave that customer either 25 percent off his or her next order or, in extreme cases, offered to redo the entire job for free.

Let Employees
Do The Work

From Marlene Rossman

If you're targeting minority markets, look to your employees for help. Is your work force multicultural? Ask employees for advice on going after the markets they know. Involve them in planning your advertising campaigns and promotions to those markets. Let them serve as your focus group for new products and services geared to minority markets. Reward employees when their ideas pay off.

For example, one employee of a small grocery store suggested printing produce and informational signs in both Spanish and English since the clientele of the store was becoming increasingly multicultural. He also recommended the owner order a line of cooking products and ingredients that were familiar to the new major segment of their market. This effort was appreciated by the customers and inspired their loyalty. The employee was not only thanked, but promoted to a position where he was in charge of the ideas he had introduced.

225

The Outsiders

From Peter Connolly

There seems to be one guiding principle most successful businesspeople agree on: Use the best external resources. When selecting your outside help, always hire the best available. If ever the rule "Don't be penny-wise and pound-foolish" was important, it's here.

From something as critical as hiring a CPA to help with your financial matters, to making sure the person handling your computer and electronic hookups is experienced and reputable, go with the best people you can afford. This is especially true where marketing issues are concerned. Don't try to design your own logo, letterhead and promotional pieces unless you're in the graphics business. You probably would have about as much success as you would filling your own cavities. Get help from people who are pros and learn from them.

226

People Power

From Michel Roux

What's a sure-fire recipe for success? Surround yourself with the best, most talented people, and infuse them with enthusiasm and vision. Nurturing a staff so that they are excited about working with you and pumped up about your business counts as one of your greatest assets. Including outside consultants can also keep your business on target. However, be sure you're getting counsel as assurance, not insurance. If you use a consultant, you're getting assurance in what you're doing so you feel more comfortable. But if you fail, no one else is going to take the blame for it.

These days, a number of small businesses are calling on the services of technology consultants. Why? Because no segment of the business universe is changing as fast as information and communications technology. It's no longer enough to simply have a phone installed. Even companies with only one or two employees realize that they can operate on the same playing field as the big guys if they have the proper communications and data systems setup. So take the time to talk to a communications consultant before you invest in a ton of equipment.

227

All Aboard!

From Peter Connolly

Prospects shouldn't be the only target for your marketing efforts. You need to market internally as well. Even the best strategies will not be maximized if your entire organization is not on board. Investing time in educating workers and communicating your strategies will optimize your efforts. If your employees don't know your goals and objectives, they can't possibly convey those to customers. When everyone in your company is in the loop, your entire staff will be contributing to your marketing efforts instead of just you.

The owner of a small floral company worked with his staff on the subject of a company philosophy before he ever opened his doors. He explained his take on the topic and then asked for their input. Together, they came up with a mission and a customer-service philosophy they all could live with and understand. They've continued to get together to regularly update each other on how things are working and to share success stories. Lots of rewards are doled out, too.

228

References Available
On Request

From Ruth Owades

Your vendors are an important part of your business—in many ways as important as your employees. And like employees, vendors need to be dependable, timely, reliable and available when you need them. If a vendor fails to deliver quality goods on time, you're left holding the bag and customers will think you are unreliable. Always make sure vendors are on the up-and-up by checking their references. It's always surprising how many people don't even bother to look into references.

A company that manufactures customized display cabinets had grown to the point where it could no longer efficiently package items for shipping. So when it was time to incorporate an outside vendor for this service, the owner not only requested bids but did some on-site visits at other businesses to see just how good the products were. He also talked with managers and employees from other companies and got firsthand information and feedback.

229

Go By The Script

From Martin R. Baird

If you know what your customers are looking for, you can develop a sales script that asks them questions leading them to your product or service. Does your business help customers save time? Ask questions about what they would do if they had extra leisure time—would they spend more time with their kids or play golf? Whether you run a telemarketing operation or a retail store, your script should help your sales force close the deal. And your salespeople aren't the only ones who can benefit from a script—give a copy to everyone on your staff, including customer service and clerical employees.

For instance, if you have a company that deals in software and computer consulting services, everyone who works for you should be able to ask a few key, probing questions that can lead to a "software diagnosis and recommendation." Simple inquiries about feeling frustrated with how certain aspects of a business are run, or wondering if there isn't an easier, more reliable way to handle information flow can lead a customer directly to a purchase that can help both of you grow.

Chapter 21

Know Your Competition

It's OK To Borrow
And Steal

From Bruce Judson

There is nothing wrong with monitoring your competitors' Web sites. You may get ideas that will work for you as well. Before creating a Web site, it's imperative that you check out the competition. What do their sites look like? How do they sell? What do they offer? Are they user friendly? Are they too slow to download? See what you like and don't like. And don't limit yourself to competitors. Check out sites in various fields.

This practice really worked for a company that designs and manufactures handles and pulls for cabinets, doors and drawers. The owners visited a number of competitors' Web sites and found that most were fairly one-dimensional and pretty boring. So they decided to have fun with theirs and used a lot of puns and visuals to make things more enjoyable. Many of their products are shown in unusual settings, and graphics that link pages look like the pulls and handles they manufacture. They even went so far as having links that read "Get a handle on other options," and "Let us pull you in a new direction."

231

Two's Company

From Jack Trout and Al Ries

In the long run, every market becomes a two-horse race. Coke and Pepsi. Hertz and Avis. Everready and Duracell. Listerine and Scope. Republicans and Democrats. The list goes on. Of course, there are always several smaller players in every market. It's up to you to decide if you want to be one of the two major players or if you'd rather service a much smaller niche within a category.

Sometimes this can be a tough decision, as in the case of a construction company that was growing very fast. It was becoming one of the two largest in a community of about 100,000 people. The owner of the company, however, was not happy with the additional headaches and employee issues that came with so much growth. As a result, he opted to downsize his very successful firm and focus only on small commercial properties or custom office buildings. This simplified his life and earned him praise as the best at what he does.

232

Second Best

From Jack Trout and Al Ries

If you're shooting for second place, your strategy is determined by the leader. If 100-year-old Coke owns the older folks, Pepsi has to go for the younger ones (the "new generation"). If Heineken is a leading imported beer, then Beck's has to become the No. 1 German imported beer. As the No. 2 in the industry, you must keep a constant watch on your competition and be able to react swiftly to their moves.

This notion applies perfectly to a rafting company in the Rocky Mountains. The guys were great at what they did, but another group had locked up the No. 1 touring position a few years earlier. As a result, the No. 2 guys played up the fact that they were smaller by choice and wanted to focus on groups who were novices, had disabilities and required special arrangements, or were in need of a customized itinerary developed just for them.

233

Stay The Course

From Michel Roux

A key factor in any business or marketing effort is to stay the course. Watching the competition is important, but once you've got a bead on what others are doing, plan your work and work your plan. You shouldn't ignore the competition, nor should you get carried away with trying to second-guess what others are doing. A lot of corporations spend too much time looking at what the competition is doing. Too many people worry so much about their competitors that they forget what they are all about. Instead of becoming leaders in their industry, they become followers of the competition, and that almost guarantees that they'll never be No. 1 in their fields. If you're confident in your vision, don't go overboard with worry about your competition. Let them worry about you.

234

Know Thy Enemy

From Philip Nulman

Most successful businesspeople agree that periodically studying the competition is important because it helps you define your strategy. So how do you go about doing this? Well, one way is to post competitors' ads on a wall and do some homework. Who are they targeting? What approach are they taking? What media are they using? Which products or services are they emphasizing? Don't do this to emulate their strategies; do it to anticipate their next moves—and beat them to it.

One insurance agency that noticed a chunk of its market was going to another company decided to study the competition. The agency noticed a big change in the competition's image from previous years. The ads were now slick and professional-looking. They featured a cross section of cultural backgrounds and focused on young families. It became apparent that the ads were targeting a diverse, young-adult and family-oriented market. This information was pivotal to the agency in planning upcoming marketing efforts; it also gave valuable clues as to how to plan its next move.

235

Design Wise

From Tim Girvin

Design your product with care. Look for ways to differentiate your product using shape, design, consumer uses, simplicity and attention to detail. You should look at all your competitors to see what they are doing and come up with something different for your product. A unique design can really set your product apart from the crowd (remember the L'eggs containers in the shape of an egg?). If you don't have the creative know-how to make your product come to life, hire a designer who can realize your vision.

Suppose your company specializes in finding and packaging custom shoe-care products. Wouldn't it be appealing to your customers to have a carrying container for these products that had compartments, a handle and a laminated interior so that if anything spilled or leaked, it wouldn't bleed through and damage something? Help from a professional design firm could make this idea a reality.

Chapter 22

It's In
The Mail

236

What's A Magalog?

From Jerry Fisher

The average American household receives nearly 90 catalogs each year. Making yours stand out from the clutter takes more than good products and great photography. The solution is to create new value, freshness and anticipation for your catalog by enhancing it with problem-solving editorial content, thereby creating a "magalog"—a magazine-cum-catalog.

There is one catalog company that has perfected this technique. The catalog offers a huge variety of communications equipment—everything from headsets to systems that have video screens attached to them. Included on almost every page of the catalog is a box with a communications tip inside. And the copy isn't just bare-bones material. It even goes so far as to give a complete explanation and thorough background on whatever the topic might be. People save their catalogs because of the valuable information, as well as the product selection.

237

Isn't That Special?

From Ruth Owades

A cardinal rule for successful entrepreneurs is "find a market niche." Specialization in a product area can make you the recognized expert. If you try to compete in an entire category, your message may be so scattered that customers will flock to other companies that specialize in niches within your category. You can't be everything to everybody. Be happy being everything to a few people.

A case in point: Years ago a woman who retired from a major corporation decided she wanted to have a home-based business. Years of fighting a hectic commute had convinced her there must be a better way. One day as she sat at home just playing with her two cats, she came upon the notion that she could develop a cat catalog from the comfort of her own couch. And that's just what she did. Her catalog appealed to cat lovers from coast to coast, and now she has customers all over the world while she operates out of her home office.

238

Full House

From Ruth Owades

I f you are in the mail order business, feature a complete product line with at least 75 to 100 items that represent your catalog's theme. You should have a full product line, otherwise your catalog can look skimpy, which in turn makes your business look amateurish. The more products you have to choose from, the bigger and more "legitimate" your company appears to customers.

Think back to the cat catalog example. While the niche is narrowly defined, the product line is broad and appealing. From antique replicas to zippered cat carryalls, the catalog covered the subject in an entertaining and colorful way.

239

Be On Your Toes

From Maxwell Sroge

The secret to mail order success can be summed up in two words: Deliver fast. We have become a very impatient society; when we want things, we want them now. We'd rather pay a premium for instant mashed potatoes than make them from scratch. So when someone calls you and says "Send me that dress I saw in your catalog," that person wants it that minute. The closer you can get to "that minute," the happier the customer will be. Offer options such as overnight, two-day air and three-day ground delivery. Even if you slap a premium on rush orders, customers will pony up the cash to get their goods fast.

240

Cost Controls

From Ruth Owades

In the mail order catalog business, you need to aim for an average sale of at least $30. You may think that selling thousands of pieces of a low-priced item will rack up profits, but in reality, processing a lot of $5 orders can put you out of business. Be aware of your costs, including shipping, packaging, catalog production and overhead. Price your products accordingly and always train your sales reps to up-sell—when customers call in to order an item, make sure the rep informs them of any specials or suggests other merchandise that would complement their original selection.

A prominent department store that does a huge volume in catalog sales trains its telephone operators to look at the catalog page that features the item the caller wants. It's not only a good way to verify selection but allows the operator to mention any of the accessories or complementary items that are shown.

241

Inventory Info

From Ruth Owades

Just as you should offer a complete product line if you're going to run a mail order business, you should also have an inventory of at least 25 percent of all the items you expect to sell. If you let your inventory run dry and can't deliver in a timely manner, your customers may run to another vendor. The faster you can get customers their merchandise, the better customers they will be.

One mail order company that primarily sells hand-knit items like sweaters found out in a hurry what an impact having limited inventory can be. No one realized that many mail order customers start doing their holiday shopping in the middle of the summer, and when there wasn't adequate stock on hand, orders disappeared. It was a tough lesson that didn't have to be repeated the following year; the company also made special note of it in the catalog copy.

242

Get Your M&Ms

From Maxwell Sroge

The basic rules for success in direct marketing are summed up in the name of a well-known candy: M&Ms. One "M" stands for identifying a *market*; the other stands for the *merchandise*. Your market must be a strong one that has shown a willingness to buy through mail order, and your merchandise must be unique and of top-notch quality. Without these two elements, you cannot have a successful catalog business.

A perfect example of this M&M theory comes from a man whose catalog features high-quality gardening tools. His research indicates that people who are sophisticated, devoted gardeners don't like to waste valuable "outdoor" time running from store to store to find just the right tool or piece of equipment. Consequently, they will let their shopping be done via the phone so they can spend more time doing what they love—gardening! In addition, they are the kind of people who work their tools with enthusiasm, so the quality has to be first-rate. The people and the products are a splendid combination and just right for the mail order market.

243

Priced To Sell

From Ruth Owades

I f you're serious about your mail order business, remember to offer a product selection with a broad price range. The wider your price range, the more customers you'll attract. Lower-priced items can be a good way to introduce customers to your product, then as their incomes grow, so will their purchases. Note, too, that a higher price often gives the impression that something is more valuable and therefore more desirable, so don't underprice by default. There are certain key price points in every merchandise line. Be sensitive to your industry and your customer.

A catalog company that features fine jewelry includes some pieces that are either high-quality costume items or are small, less expensive versions of the pricier pieces. The catalog displays pieces in all price ranges with equal attention to detail, and the items arrive in lovely packages no matter how inexpensive they might be. You never know—some day the people who only dabbled on the fringes through lower priced purchases might be able to afford the high-end items.

244

Where Are Your Values?

From Maxwell Sroge

Never underestimate the importance of providing good values. People are looking for low prices, but they also want a certain degree of quality. Low prices for low-quality items that won't last or won't work don't present a good value. By the same token, high-quality items that come with a stiff sticker price don't represent true value. The key is to present merchandise that represents a good value; value is the right combination of quality, features and price.

A good way to gauge whether or not you have the right combination of quality, features and price is, of course, to check out the competition before you set your catalog in stone. If you're going to be selling office supplies, do some comparison work and be selective about what you offer. People get more than one catalog featuring the same items and you can bet they do price comparisons. Even a dollar or two difference in price, coupled with a nicer photo layout, can make a big difference in influencing opinions.

245

Stop Hunting, Start Nurturing

From Maxwell Sroge

Realize that nothing is more valuable than an existing customer. In direct marketing especially, success is predicated exclusively on the buying activity of your established customers. You cannot run a successful direct-marketing business if you are constantly having to find new customers. It's too expensive. You have to nurture your existing customers. Keep in touch with them, let them know about special promotions and sales, and even offer specials that are available only to existing customers. The more you can convince customers that they are important to you, the more likely they will remain customers. In a good direct-marketing company, the customer list will generate three to five times greater response than a prospect list.

246

Weighty Issues

From Maxwell Sroge

Create a catalog with a minimum of 24 pages. A catalog must have a certain "heft" to receive attention in the mailbox. Remember, your catalog will be competing against hundreds of others, including the likes of *J. Crew, Victoria's Secret* and other standbys. Your catalog can easily get lost in the shuffle if it's too thin.

Bear in mind, also, that if you come up with only a minimum number of pages, you might be premature in launching your mail order business. If you have only enough items to fill 20 pages, then you probably need to explore how you can expand what you're offering. A complete product line and ample versions and sizes of what you feature are essential to competition in the mail order race. Ask yourself, too, if you're trying to economize by featuring too many items on a page. The images can look distorted and amateurish if they're crammed onto each page. White space and high-quality photos or illustrations give a look of quality and success to your publication.

247

Give 'Em The Easy Way Out

From Maxwell Sroge

Make it easy for your customers to do business with your mail order operation. Consumers respond to companies that make life easier for them—via clear catalog descriptions, good photographs and an easy-to-order/easy-to-return process. They won't work too hard to decipher what you are trying to communicate. Your order-taking process should also be quick and simple. Offer as many ways as possible for customers to send orders: fax, phone, mail, e-mail and the Web. On the phones, don't make customers wait on hold for several minutes. Have enough employees to handle the calls.

Also take heed of the folks who thought they didn't need to provide an 800 number for their customers. They offered terrific mail order photo albums and storage containers. They had wonderful people working their phones, and delivery was reliable. They noticed, however, that their growth was slow. So when they asked their callers what they could do better, they were told time and again, "Get an 800 number." They did and business skyrocketed.

248

D-Base Drills

From Maxwell Sroge

Maintain an excellent database. The key to the success of any mail order catalog business is what information you send to which customers. The more you know about your customers, the better off you will be. For example, if you sell computers, you need to know whether your customers use PCs or Macintosh systems; whether they network or use stand-alone computers; whether they have portable computers and so on. Having this information in your database helps you target them with information that's of interest to them.

This was the turning point for the owners of a women's apparel company. Once they acquired a database that tracked size and style orders, they were able to expand their offerings by customizing their catalogs to accommodate women who wore larger sizes. They developed a catalog filled with the styles these women liked best and mailed it directly to them.

23

Homebased
Hints

249

Our Little Secret

From Jeanne Koester

One of the greatest concerns of many clients is confidentiality. In big companies with hundreds of employees, customer confidentiality is difficult to maintain—faxes are often read by people other than the recipient, and access to computer files and customer lists can translate into a lot of people knowing a customer's vitals. Market your confidentiality and you may see your customer list expand. The small size of homebased businesses can be marketed as a strength in terms of ensuring potential customers that when it comes to their business, mum's the word.

In fact, you can take this notion and apply it to all your areas of communication. From your fax forms to your voice-messaging system, you can play up the fact that what comes to you stays with you.

250

Target Your Own Kind

From Jeanne Koester

Homebased entrepreneurs should channel some of their marketing efforts to other homebased entrepreneurs. They understand the challenges you've been through and are often happy to use your services. Find fellow homebased business owners through associations for homebased business owners or by advertising in magazines geared to homebased entrepreneurs.

This philosophy is not only considerate but a wise way to collaborate and partner with other companies. Networking, referrals and even business orders can be generated from a desire to be supportive of other hardworking homebased entrepreneurs.

251

Flex Appeal

From Jeanne Koester

As a homebased business owner, you have one major advantage over the big guys: flexibility. Take advantage of it. You set your own hours, so take advantage of cheaper phone and fax rates. Make phone calls to Europe and the East Coast at 5 a.m., to the West Coast at night; the rates will be cheaper and you may actually catch people in the office. Fax at midnight—you'll save money and ensure your message is the first thing customers see in the morning. Also use flexibility as a selling point: Working on rush jobs or doing an occasional overnight turnaround is something you can offer to special clients or when you want to get someone's business.

Consider, for example, one fellow who does independent media buying for people who want to advertise on radio and television. When a client called him on Saturday with an urgent request to get something on the air for the Fourth of July holiday coming up on Wednesday, the other advertising agencies were tripped up because it was a weekend. But the homebased buyer said "The weekends are no problem." He had the voice-over script, copy and a sample schedule ready to go by Monday morning.

252

Take The Lead

From Jeanne Koester

omebased business owners are still fighting credibility problems with some people who equate a homebased business with a hobby. Make sure customers and others in the business community know that you're serious about what you do.

To gain respect in the business community, get out of the house—and get known. If you position yourself as a leader, you get more publicity. Taking a leadership role in your chamber of commerce, networking group or trade association ensures that your company's name shows up frequently on the organization's letterhead, press releases and anything else sent to the community.

One woman who runs her regional calendar service from her home happens to be a world-class civic volunteer. She's articulate and smart. She's willing to be a spokesperson for various causes and manages to fit everything in because of her homebased setup. She also has an ear open for other things going on or being planned and that allows her to beef up her calendar.

253

Dial "M" For Motivate

From Jeanne Koester

Homebased entrepreneurs have to work harder at staying motivated than those in larger businesses. In big companies, co-workers can help stimulate ideas and stir motivation. To keep yourself out of the doldrums, you need to get out of the house. Attend seminars, workshops and conferences—whether they're directly related to your industry or if they cover general business matters. Meet and network with others in your industry to share ideas and discuss how to overcome problems. Keep abreast of changes in your field by reading trade journals, newsletters and other publications. Staying active in the business community and in your industry can provide the oomph to keep you on your toes.

Chapter 24

Go
Global

254

Sell The American Dream

From Eileen Cassidy

Know the value of "Made in America." The "USA" name retains tremendous selling power in much of the world, so promote your company and products as American. Put a "Made in America" label on all products and tout the fact that your company is U.S.-based in all your written communications, marketing materials and ads.

This tactic has really paid off for one company that makes hiking and camping gear. The owners knew there were large markets in Europe and South America for their kind of products, but their gear didn't get much notice until they added a colorful embroidered tag to all their products that reads "Made in the USA."

255

The Price Is Right

From Eileen Cassidy

Pricing your product for sale internationally involves more than pricing for domestic sales. Develop an international pricing strategy. Take into consideration all the factors involved with exporting, including shipping and tariffs. Be aware, too, that most currencies fluctuate in value, sometimes dramatically, and not all currencies are readily convertible. Keeping this in mind before you set a price will help prevent losses from underpricing your products.

You might also want to do an informal survey of other comparable companies that do business in the countries you're targeting. Find out their experiences with pricing and get a feel for what you need to prepare for.

256

Money Talks

From Eileen Cassidy

You are probably well aware that taking your product abroad requires capital. Fortunately, there are numerous financing channels available to help you in your exporting efforts. Get up to speed on export finance. Meet your local banker and ask about programs available to finance your product or service abroad. Also ask about the Small Business Administration's Export Working Capital Program—it's available nationwide.

A fellow who owns a company that manufactures extremely durable yet lightweight garage doors knew there was a need for them in Southeast Asia. He also knew there was a huge labor pool there and that these items could be produced and delivered inexpensively. He did his homework, prepared an impressive presentation and won over a group of venture capitalists.

257

Get The Legal Lowdown

From Eileen Cassidy

Exporters often run afoul when it comes to legalese, especially since it's foreign legalese. The best way to avoid legal snafus is to know the laws before you begin the exporting process. When you're starting out, tariffs, regulations and distributorship agreements can be intimidating. Get answers before you stumble into a legal thicket.

The Export Legal Assistance Network can help you overcome these hurdles; call the SBA's Answer Desk at (800) 8-ASK-SBA for more information. You might also want to do some informal investigating by talking to other successful companies that have done business in the areas you're interested in.

258

Going Global

From Eileen Cassidy

Taking your product abroad? Get smart about foreign competition before you unleash your product in another country. Become familiar with the local marketplace, business environment and economic conditions. Hit up local trade offices for information and statistics on demographics and buying patterns. Know who your competitors are, what they do that works and what they do that doesn't sell. This will save you money in the long run.

A small firm that makes a line of unique hair-care products found out from doing just this kind of research that in the country where the owners were going to market their products, packages in certain colors simply turned people off. It seems that a company that had broached this country earlier with its line of cosmetics couldn't sell much of anything because the packages were almost completely white, a color that signified death to potential customers.

259

We Aren't In Kansas Anymore

From Eileen Cassidy

When dealing with international markets, one rule prevails: Be flexible. Remember, the American way isn't the only way. Be sensitive to other countries' cultures, and adapt your product or service accordingly. Your marketing and advertising efforts must also be geared specifically to specific markets.

When a large-animal veterinarian decided his consulting business should expand to countries in South America, he wisely began studying the cultures of those countries. He and his employees took classes in Spanish and Portuguese, met with an expert on doing business internationally, made a number of site visits, and took time to interview several executives who were already doing work in those countries. The last thing he wanted to do was inadvertently step on anyone's toes, or hooves!

260

Futureworld

From Eileen Cassidy

Our world is anything but static. Today's economic powerhouses may not be dominant marketplaces in the future. So don't limit your marketing horizons to those countries that make up today's strongest economic markets. Exporters should look for opportunities in the world's growing markets. As pinpointed by the Commerce Department, these include Argentina, The Association of Southeast Asian Nations, Brazil, China, India, Mexico, Poland, South Africa, South Korea and Turkey. By 2010, these emerging markets will account for 25 percent of the world's imports. By getting in on the action now, you can look forward to a share of that percentage.

261

Don't Give Up

From Eileen Cassidy

Bear in mind that exporting is a process, not a transaction. You need to be in it for the long haul to reap the rewards. Don't expect to be able to go into a country, make a quick killing and get out. It just doesn't happen that way. When things get tough, stick with it.

One company that exports machinery for sewage treatment plants knew there would be a market for its products internationally but had to wait for some countries to get their infrastructure ready for the products that were available. With hard work and patience, the U.S. company assisted a number of other countries in upgrading their sewage systems so that the machinery being exported would be suitable for use.

262

Stay Slim

From Richard Kirshenbaum and Jonathan Bond

If you're planning to take your product or service global, think small. No matter how many markets you're planning to enter, cut that number in half. International marketing takes more time and resources than you think. With customs restrictions, import and export laws, financial exchange rates and language and cultural differences, your international marketing plan may not go as smoothly as you think. So pare down your plans—it's better to succeed in five markets than to fail in 10.

This lesson was learned quickly by a clothing manufacturer who attempted to market her line of resortwear to dozens of warm-weather countries. The process became overwhelming, and so did the cost. When she pared down her choices to about a half dozen countries in the same geographic area, it became more like getting her arms around a puppy than an elephant.

263

Don't Go It Alone

From Richard Kirshenbaum and Jonathan Bond

If you don't have a strong partner in an international market, think twice before entering it alone. Co-branding has become an effective way for companies to expand their presence. Partners in the country you're targeting can provide you with invaluable assistance—they already know the language, the culture, the community, the customers and their buying habits. It could take you years of market research and thousands of dollars before you could acquire that knowledge on your own. So team up and take advantage of their know-how.

One entrepreneur who wanted to provide a software package designed especially for hospital use knew his chances of success would increase if he had a partner already in the technology field in the country he was targeting. He made several trips abroad and interviewed three different communications firms. In the long run, the time and money he invested in this research paid off a thousandfold when an entire chain of hospitals bought into the concept on his first visit.

264

Eat A Piece Of
Humble Pie

From Richard Kirshenbaum and Jonathan Bond

Don't be arrogant. You may have made a name for yourself and your company stateside, but that doesn't mean a thing to foreign consumers. You need to adjust your attitude when you go overseas; don't assume your reputation precedes you. You'll need to start all over in terms of gaining the trust of foreign consumers and in building a reputation for your business.

The owners of a successful environmental consulting firm from the United States stubbed their toes when they started doing business in Japan. Because they were so excited about their opportunities there, and because they were also under a real time crunch, they carried that sense of urgency with them into meetings and site visits. They pressured people for decisions, failed to develop personal relationships and did a bit too much bragging about their reputation. As a result, they lost the deal and had to take solace in what they had learned from their mistakes.

265

Go Guerrilla

From Richard Kirshenbaum and Jonathan Bond

You generally have less prestige and fewer resources in an overseas market, so strategize accordingly. Get creative and find ways to bring attention to your business that don't cost you a bundle. And remember, what works in the United States won't necessarily be a hit abroad.

For instance, when General Motors introduced its successful Chevy Nova in South America, the company couldn't figure out why it wasn't selling. When it discovered "nova" means "it won't go," the company quickly renamed the car "Caribe" in its Spanish-speaking markets.

266

The Choice Is Yours

From Richard Kirshenbaum and Jonathan Bond

Just because somebody wants to distribute your product in another country doesn't mean you should let him or her—you could end up working with a scam artist or someone who doesn't know what he or she is doing.

It may never have occurred to you before that your product or service would have international appeal, so don't let the notion that you could go global turn your head. Flattering though an offer may be, *you* should select the partner and market, not the reverse. That means you need to do your homework and investigate potential partners—speak to their clients, vendors and even their competitors to get a clear picture of their reliability and potential for success. Only when you feel confident that they'll make the grade should you enter into a partnership or joint marketing venture.

267

When In Rome . . .

From Richard Kirshenbaum and Jonathan Bond

As an international marketer, you need to change your mind-set. Before you can get past the business barrier of operating in another country, you must get over the emotional one. We're taught that America is the best country in the world and the best place to do business. But go overseas with that attitude and you'll likely get an icy reception from your target market, which means your business is almost sure to fail. You must train yourself to think with an export mentality, like smaller countries do, to compete in a global marketplace. Don't expect foreign consumers to adapt to the American way; you've got to adapt to their way of doing things.

One of the most frequently misunderstood areas for adaptation has to do with punctuality. While many people from other countries do not adhere to being somewhere "on the dot," you still will be expected to show up promptly. That's where your export mentality must take over and allow you to feel OK about having to wait.

268

All Foreigners Are Not Created Equal

From Richard Kirshenbaum and Jonathan Bond

Global marketers need to think psychographically, not just geographically. Don't make the mistake of assuming that all Europeans fall into one homogeneous group or that all Asians have the same buying patterns. Every foreign market is filled with a wide variety of people, income levels, interests and needs. Upscale travelers from different countries often have more in common with each other than with their fellow countrymen. For instance, New York City and London are more alike than New York City and Phoenix.

When doing business in India for the first time, a company that manufactures furniture made from recycled plastic discovered that the variety in buying patterns and negotiating styles varied enormously from state to state and dialect to dialect. A one-size-fits-all approach didn't work, so they spent several weeks consulting with businesspeople from each market region, learning how to customize their language and approach for each area.

269

Be Un-American

From Richard Kirshenbaum and Jonathan Bond

Take some time-honored advice from international experts and resist the familiar. When selling to foreign markets, don't assume that it's smart to hire an American or push the products that sell best in the United States. Be conscious of your national biases, and recognize when you are letting them influence your decisions. At first, you may have difficulty knowing when your Americanness is getting in the way of smart marketing but the more international marketing you do, the easier it will be for you to determine when you are being "too American."

One company from the United States that does business in other countries insists that its executives not only learn as much of the language as possible but also regularly attend cultural events, ceremonial activities or performances that further enhance their knowledge of that country and reduce their tendency to be "too American."

270

Home Is No. 1

From Richard Kirshenbaum and Jonathan Bond

Think regionally before you think globally. Experienced exporters strongly recommend perfecting your business at home before you take the leap overseas. That way, you can work out the kinks in manufacturing, design and product development before getting entangled in dealings with foreign markets. Service businesses should follow the same guidelines and perfect their business skills domestically before heading overseas.

Consider, for instance, the difference between doing business in the northeast part of the United States vs. the South. The pace, the level of familiarity, the language variances and the sheer expanse of territory all can influence how you approach and deal with widely different populations. If you can master the United States from coast to coast, you just might be ready for the world.

271

Fair Game

From Richard Kirshenbaum and Jonathan Bond

Learn foreign countries' perceptions of fair play. You may be surprised to learn that what is considered a corrupt business practice in the United States may be accepted as legal in another country. And if you don't make those actions part of your business dealings abroad, you may lose out on customers. Knowing what is fair game in other countries will help level the playing field if you are competing with local businesses for customers.

For instance, in some Pacific Rim countries, offering a visiting executive something bizarre and mysterious to eat is not only acceptable, but may be a sort of test to see just how determined and committed the visitor is to making a deal work. In the United States, serving items that are extremely unfamiliar or odd would be considered totally inappropriate and unkind.

Chapter 25

Major In
Minorities

272

Minor In Marketing

From Marlene Rossman

Marketers need to reach out to all customers with respect and relevance regardless of race, nationality or ethnicity. Making a cultural, racial or ethnic mistake means you may never recover in that marketplace. Do your homework to find out what appeals to different markets and what is viewed as offensive or insulting. That will help you avoid costly blunders.

One advertising agency learned this the hard way when it generated a series of ads for a home builder that depicted Chinese, Japanese and Korean people all grouped together. The individual groups felt they were not being spoken to directly and ultimately were insulted by the message.

273

Take The Easy Route

From Marlene Rossman

When searching out groups to sell to, don't make it harder for yourself. Cast a wide net, but understand that some groups—for instance, recent arrivals from China who have settled in New York City's Chinatown—often are insular and difficult to reach. But don't give up; just pursue other groups that are more open. This may require some trial and error on your part, but always use common sense when choosing what groups are most likely to respond to your efforts.

An art dealer in a large city realized that many of his patrons and neighbors were African-American. As he grew to know his customers better, he realized that he not only had a chance to learn more about African-American art and artists, but that he also had a great marketing opportunity ahead of him. As a result of carrying more paintings, sculptures and prints that reflected the African-American culture, his business increased in all areas.

274

Getting To Know You

From Marlene Rossman

Even insular ethnic groups can be an excellent source of business if approached correctly. Relationship building is key; create trust before trying to sell. For many ethnic groups, this can take twice as long compared with selling to mainstream populations. Don't get discouraged. If you are aware of this from the get-go, you'll budget the correct amount of time and money to your efforts. And if you stick with it, you'll discover the payoff is that once you sell to these groups, you'll have very loyal customers.

For example, when a huge influx of immigrants from Indochina started pouring into the area, a community college made every attempt to focus on education, literacy and achievement in its ads in an effort to respond to the cultural tendencies of that group. The ad copy read "Achieve the American dream . . . read, study, succeed." The college administrators knew these characteristics were highly valued in the culture they were targeting, and they made sure they had bilingual employees available to help counsel the people who responded to their ads.

275

On The Home Front

From Marlene Rossman

If you already sell internationally, leverage those successes to sell domestically. For example, if you're selling to Latin America, build on that success and go after domestic Latinos. You will find that many of the techniques you use abroad will work stateside as well. Sure, there are differences between the groups, but know-how picked up abroad can definitely be applied here.

To be specific, you might want to play to the fact that Latino cultures place a high emphasis on the family. Make sure your ads show family activities, such as people shopping together, rather than a lone customer. If this approach works in another country, then it might be especially effective at home.

276

Viva La Difference

From Marlene Rossman

It's important to remember that marketing to ethnic and minority markets doesn't mean marketing to a homogeneous group. To be successful, you need to be aware of subsegment differences. For instance, all Latinos aren't the same. An innocent word to Mexican-Americans may be an obscenity to Puerto Ricans. A product that's a hit with African-Americans may flop with blacks from Jamaica. Don't fall into the trap of lumping people.

A case in point: In San Francisco, the Chinese population is likely to appreciate promptness and precision. Ethnic Malays, however, have a looser concept of time, and marketing to them may call for a more relaxed approach.

277

Spend Smarter, Not More

From Marlene Rossman

Marketing to minorities has its advantages. Advertising through multicultural media is less expensive than mainstream media, and those audiences are very loyal to advertisers. That's great news, but don't think that you can just take mainstream ads and place them in media geared to your target market. Make the effort to create relevant lifestyle ads for each market. What it will cost you in time and money to create will pay off in additional sales because it speaks directly to your market.

When a telecommunications company attempted to introduce a new product to its customers, a video was produced to help illustrate its features. The glitch came when it was shown to a sizeable American-Indian population living in small to midsized communities in the Southwest. In a region that is known for its casual, more relaxed lifestyle, the video production company totally blew it with its hyper-talking, sophisticated-dressing cast members trying to make a pitch to an audience that was on a different plane entirely.

278

Forget The Token Efforts

From Marlene Rossman

To market successfully to minority groups, outreach must be consistent and long term. Don't spend big dollars on Cinco de Mayo and expect larger payoffs—unless you follow up with sincere marketing year-round. The best way to build a following among minority markets is to keep your message in front of your consumers through a variety of media outlets.

This can be done through messages on non-English-speaking radio stations or stations known to have a large minority listenership. It can also come through ads and features in weekly newspapers published by and for leading minority groups.

Chapter 26

Great
Updates

279

New And Different!

From Diane Perlmutter

Don't rest on your laurels. Just because you came up with a killer product or service doesn't mean you can sit back and watch the cash roll in for the rest of your life. Whatever it is you sell—whether it's a product or a service—it has to stay in step with your customers and a changing society. Marketers should be encouraged to regularly evaluate their product or service to ensure it is still priced, packaged and designed right. Continual improvement is the best way to keep customers coming back.

Updating its packaging made all the difference to a company that manufactures cleaning products. The package went from a vintage 1950s look to a more modern appearance with a glistening label and a sleeker bottle. This change made a huge difference, and within the first six weeks of its debut, profits were showing a 15 percent increase.

280

Start At The Top

From Leann Anderson

Getting the ear of the CEO can sometimes be a great way to *tell* and *sell.* If you want a decision to be made quickly and decisively, going to the top may be the most direct route to success. Just be sure you do it in a way that respects the individual's time, gets to the heart of the matter, and tells your story in a positive way.

For instance, take a lesson from the company that noticed many firms were experiencing a high level of employee absenteeism during the cold and flu season. These manufacturers of an antibacterial hand gel knew that bacteria and germs were frequently transmitted by people who were unable to wash their hands as often as they would like. So the company sent kits to several hundred CEOs and cleverly boxed them with a label reading "Anti-germ warfare." Inside were tissues, hard candy and samples of the gel, along with an explanation of how stopping the spread of germs could decrease employee absenteeism. Going to the top in this case definitely got the message across.

281

Churn, Baby, Churn

From Guy Kawasaki

Don't overlook the importance of constantly keeping in motion. Once you ship your product, the winners and losers are determined not so much by where your product is as by how fast you're improving it. Never stop making your products better. And if you do find a way to significantly refine your product once it has hit the market, think of the marketing push you'll get out of touting the fact that it's "new and improved!"

A great example of staying in motion comes from a company in Japan that manufactures bathroom fixtures. The owners realized they were losing market share to their competition and asked themselves what they could do to set their company apart. After all, a toilet is a toilet, right? Wrong. They decided to add value to their toilet by designing a fixture that not only served as a basic utility piece, but provided diagnostic information as well. From their toilet came an analysis of body fluids and weight levels that provides information on such things as a person's body fat, blood pressure and blood sugar level.

282

When Old Is New Again

From Jerry Fisher

Repackage your goods. Big profits can come from taking an existing product and repackaging it into something new that you can sell to customers. Magazine and newsletter publishers do this kind of repackaging all the time. For instance, people who market specialized newsletters are enticing prospects all the time with free "special reports" that seem at least as valuable, in terms of information, as the newsletter—if not more so. The goal of the marketing effort is to sell the prospect on getting all this incredibly helpful information free of charge and— oh, by the way—it's yours just for trying out our little ol' newsletter for 30 days. The information in the special reports is drawn from previous newsletter issues, so they're relatively cheap and easy to produce.

283

Keep It Fresh

From Diane Perlmutter

Don't be afraid to innovate. Stay on top of trends and don't be hesitant to be the first to try something new. Trends often start with one group or in a particular region and then spread to others. In our youth-oriented culture, many trends start with teens and twentysomethings, so keep an eye on what high school and college students are doing. To stay in the loop, set your dial to MTV, hang out at a mall, surf the Net and read magazines geared to the younger set. Once you spot a new trend, find a way for your business to capitalize on it.

In one community, a restaurateur noticed that his teenagers were desperate for a place to go to hang out and dance. Numerous clubs existed for the 21-and-over crowd, but there wasn't anything for 14- to 18-year-olds. So he opened several spots where kids could socialize, dance and play high-tech games. The surroundings were modest, the overhead was low and the hours were designed to fit school night and weekend schedules.

284

Don't Get Stale

From Tim Girvin

With the passage of time, your product may need refreshing. Is it time to change your product color, to look at more inventive ways to describe your product, or to liven up your point-of-purchase display? Depending on the market, some brands can last for 30 years or more, while others barely last five. Some industries are changing so quickly (think technology) that products need constant updating just to keep in step with the market. Keep this in mind when you're budgeting for product development and marketing. How will you know when your product's no longer passing muster? Stay in contact with consumers, and use testing or customer reviews to see if your strategy is still working. If it's not, it's time to change.

285

Theory Of Evolution

From Michel Roux

In business, it's imperative that you constantly evolve, change and reinvent yourself. That's what life is all about. That doesn't necessarily mean you must change a great product or a great idea, but you can improve it with new techniques. For example, if your print advertising campaign reels in a host of new customers, try taking that same campaign concept and placing ads on the Internet. Conversely, you may want to stick with an advertising medium that has worked for you in the past and test new concepts. The basic idea: If it ain't broke, don't fix it; instead, build on something that's already working for you.

Take, for example, a jewelry store that had a lock on several billboard locations. For years the store's owners prided themselves in coming up with traffic-stoppers for showing off their designs. About a year ago, they realized these ads were perfect for the backs or sides of buses, park benches or even the tops or sides of delivery vans used by a local florist.

Chapter 27

Be A
Trend
Tracker

286

True Value

From Watts Wacker

In the future, value will be based less on price and more on dimensions. Value marketing was originally about getting price back in line, then it became the relationship between quality and price, and then the intersection of dimensions like time and stress. Another factor in value is situation. If you find yourself in the situation of being an unknowledgeable shopper, particularly about things like electronics or high-tech equipment, you will pay a premium to find someone who knows what he or she is talking about—even for low-end merchandise.

One fellow realized this when he started his "cell doctor" service. He travels from place to place and person to person, helping people program their new personal communication service phones. From speed dial to call forwarding to paging features, he knows 'em all, and people who are in a hurry will pay handsomely to have him make their start-up as painless as possible.

287

Home On The Road

From Watts Wacker

The notion of home is going to become a concept. Home is no longer about location; it's about having that feeling of home wherever you go. To succeed in the hospitality, travel and auto industries, marketers will have to find ways to make their clients' business trips and vacations include a little bit of home. Cars, trucks and other modes of transportation will have to take on more characteristics of home—television monitors, on-board computers and more. The way marketers advertise their products and services may emphasize the comforts of home.

One highly successful bookstore made its mark on the national scene because it was the first to offer overstuffed chairs, lamps and end tables in a living roomlike setting right in the midst of the store. This gesture enticed people to take a load off, sit down and relax with a good book.

288

The New Private Eyes

From Watts Wacker

The future of retailing is not about bricks and mortar. It's about transaction management and who owns the data. By 2010—but we're also seeing the beginnings of it now—we'll all have personal privacy consultants, and they will play three roles: Like a sheriff, they will protect us; like an editor, they will make sure we find out only the things we want; and like an agent, they will make sure we get paid for the information about our lives that we make available. So if you're cooking dinner and someone calls to sell you life insurance, you will automatically be credited $10 for picking up the phone, then 50 cents per minute for hearing the pitch. You will give information about yourself because you'll get paid for it. Consumers will sell information about themselves to the highest bidder and will have a company to organize and package it for them.

289

The Sound Of Music

From Watts Wacker

It can be argued that the role of music will become immensely therapeutic. Music has many opportunities to be an energy-enhancing part of our lives, and energy is very important to the consumer right now. Marketers are already selling mood music designed to de-stress our lives, boost our energy and improve spirituality. Find ways to incorporate music into your marketing strategies or tap into the power of music with a music-based product of your own.

For example, a company that's famous for educational products took note of the research that proved IQ and test scores temporarily increased after listening to Mozart. As a result, the company now manufactures musical collections that can influence everything from test results to blood pressure.

Chapter **28**

Consistency
Counts

290

The "C" Word

From Jay Conrad Levinson

If you were wondering what makes marketing work, there's a one-word answer: commitment. Even mediocre marketing with commitment works much better than brilliant marketing without it. What exactly does commitment mean? It means making a financial promise to fund your marketing efforts, devoting the time necessary to create a solid campaign, and implementing that campaign on a consistent basis.

One young man who started out working at a municipal golf course when he was 11 has gone from *mowing* the greens to *growing* the greens. Over the years, he realized that a key to having a great golf course is the condition of the greens. He developed a company that does nothing but grow, harvest, treat, store and pamper the grasses best suited to golf greens. He's the guru of grass and has become wealthy because he consistently markets his expertise and his products. Every year he devotes 7 percent of his overall budget to *telling* and *selling*.

291

Repetition, Repetition, Repetition

From Diane Perlmutter

f you think just because your customers have already bought your product or used your service that they remember all the reasons why it's the best, you may be fooling yourself. Yes, customers may place an order after hearing your sales pitch on what makes your company stand out, but that doesn't mean they'll remember all the benefits you provide once you leave. Don't be complacent. You may think you've said it before, but you need to keep telling customers why they should continue buying from you. Consumers hear so many messages that it's important to repeat what made them buy your product or service in the first place.

In a competitive battle between two newspapers that covered a midsized city, the paper that had been around the longest continued to remind its readers and advertisers that even though its news might cost a bit more, it's never missed a day of delivering the news in 23 years. Even during a major flood, it got the paper out. Reliability was its byword.

292

Pay Up!

From Jay Conrad Levinson

When you're signing your name at the bottom of a check, marketing feels like an expense. And especially since you don't always see immediate results, you may think it's better to put out another financial fire instead of spending on marketing. But that's why you need to create ways to track responses from your ads, postcards, fliers, word-of-mouth referrals and every other tactic you use. Marketing's really an investment—the best available in America today—if you do it right.

When the owner of a small equipment rental company questioned the value of marketing, his partner (who was also his wife) suggested tracking all the marketing they did through one of their stores and cutting out the marketing for their second location. It doesn't take a genius to figure out what happened. Increased sales and business inquiries boomed at the first location while the second barely held its own. Do-it-yourself testing can be a valuable way to gain insights into how and why to market.

293

Personality Profile

From Peter Connolly

Since consumers are exposed to your brand through a variety of channels, it is imperative that each medium uphold and reinforce your brand identity. Being consistent in all communication vehicles will help you develop your brand "personality." Too many marketers don't start to think about their brand identity and what type of image they'd like to convey until after they realize their marketing campaigns aren't working. Solidify your brand identity first, before it's too late.

A roofing company that trades on the fact that it's been around for 17 years took the time to market its reliability in every medium it could afford. Its marketing materials pointed out that it wasn't the type of company that swooped down on desperate people following a hail storm. The company could be counted on to stand behind its work and could be contacted any day of the week with assurance that someone would respond to a need.

294

All Systems Go

From Rick Crandall

Service providers in particular often get caught up in their work and neglect to market. This can become a vicious circle. Because they don't market systematically, they see spotty results, so they continue to not market systematically. Set up a routine in which you send out letters, make calls or write ad headlines for a set amount of time every morning or on certain days of the week. Service providers often find that they need to devote just as much time to marketing their services as to providing them. Chasing down new work can be time-consuming, but it's a must.

One fellow who provides training and consulting services in the areas of time management and professional development practices what he teaches. He sends an average of 25 handwritten, personal postcards a week to potential clients. He sends another 15 to former clients and makes it a point to supply some little tidbit of information to several different newspapers each month.

Chapter 29

Just Do It

295

Don't Worry, Be Crappy

From Guy Kawasaki

Companies spend way too much time and effort creating the "perfect product." But if you don't move fast, the market will pass you by. And you can be sure that a competitor will introduce a similar product first and beat you to the punch. Of course, this doesn't mean you should introduce a shoddy product that's wrought with problems. Get your product to a reasonable stage, and take a shot.

Two women wanted to start a kitchen design business, but they realized it was hard for some clients to explain what was already in place at home while sitting in an office somewhere else. As a result, they started a "kitchens on wheels" business from the back of their van. They stocked it with samples, drafting tools and tons of printed information about the materials they offered, the finishes on their cabinets, and the appliances they recommended, and off they went. While they made lots of mistakes, they considered their company a work in progress and made improvements along the way.

296

Go For The Goal

From Dan Peña

Think as large as humanly possible. It doesn't cost anything to aim high. Too many marketing people don't think big enough. For example, Ted Turner, as the marketer building CNN, wanted to develop a multimedia corporation and set goals that transcended his lifetime. In contrast, most people who attend seminars or read books or magazines about entrepreneurship are thinking on a very micro, not macro, basis. Don't limit yourself or sell yourself short. Think beyond where you want your business to be today; think about where you want it to be 10 years from now, 20 years from now, and beyond. Then create your marketing plan based on those aspirations. Your marketing needs to be as far-reaching as you want your business to be.

A family that has a secret for making great green chili took their talents to the marketplace when they opened their first restaurant. With each satisfied customer came the dream of more locations and more happy customers. Their vision took them beyond the safe and predictable, and now they have 13 locations.

297

Do-It-Yourself Marketing

From Leann Anderson

You shouldn't leave all your marketing research to the professionals. But neither should you try to do it all yourself. Trouble surfaces when the balance between professional know-how and personal common sense is lost. Instead, look for areas where the pros can truly be of help to you. This might come in the form of doing some survey work that requires formal design and follow-up. You simply may not have the time or personnel to do a thorough job of surveying your customer base. Instead, you might be more suited to conducting informal focus groups or customer roundtables, especially if you know your customers personally. It's likely they would appreciate being able to tell you something face to face. Only you know exactly what you want your research to tell you, so you definitely need to be involved.

298

Balancing Act

From Leann Anderson

The key thing to remember when it comes to do-it-yourself marketing is to look for balance. Two of the most frequently made marketing mistakes are: 1) jumping into a venture without doing any research, and 2) suffering from paralysis by analysis, whereby people spend so much time analyzing and examining every possible outcome that opportunity and the competition pass them by. Try not to find yourself in either camp. Do something while you are researching and talking to the pros, even if it is only a postcard sent to everyone within your local ZIP code. Just don't spend every cent you have on a wild advertising campaign before you've talked to some experts.

Take time to honestly appraise your own research abilities. You may discover you need help. Remember, market research can be successful when the partnership involves people who know the methods and know the customers.

299

Basic Instinct

From Michel Roux

The secret to successful marketing? Go with your gut. Sometimes business owners get so wrapped up in market research, focus groups, forecasts and statistics that they lose sight of their own ideas. Going with your instincts ensures you won't overdo or underdo what's necessary to reach your goals. At the same time, you have to temper your instinct with common sense.

Years ago a woman who worked for an orthopedic surgeon saw hundreds of patients coming in with back, knee and leg problems. Frequently, these were the result of wearing bad shoes and not exercising properly. Before anyone was into power walking, she knew instinctively that people would need to change their bad habits. So she opened a store specializing in walking shoes and gear. They said she was crazy, but her gut said "Go for it." Today, she's happy and successful with a whole chain of stores.

300

Get A Life Cycle

From Guy Kawasaki

Products go through life cycles, so your marketing strategies must, too. Sometimes you need to seek niches; other times you need to ship as fast as you can. Be aware of what your product's life cycle is to be sure your marketing efforts are in sync with what your company needs. And be flexible because you have to go with the flow of your product's life cycle.

When the owners of a time-honored sporting goods company started realizing that competition was popping up all over the place, they realized that their attention to detail had overtaken their ability to respond quickly to their customers. They regrouped in a hurry and developed a plan for delivering their products twice as fast as they used to without compromising their quality.

301

Perseverance Pays Off

From Michel Roux

Be tenacious in your vision and don't be discouraged by setbacks. Setbacks aren't failure; failure is simply failing to persevere. Whatever you are doing, if you're getting any kind of results, persevere. When times get tough, you don't have to throw in the towel—you need to take a look at what went wrong and make adjustments. Often, a minor tuneup is all that's needed to get your business back on track.

The owner of a small deli found that business was slacking off. He tried new products and advertised more, but nothing helped. One day, he decided to go over his customer list and find out what most of his patrons had in common. Surprisingly, more than 60 percent of them worked at a large manufacturing plant for modular homes. The plant's management had changed and shortened the lunch hour for most employees. They simply didn't have time to visit the deli any longer. As a result of this research, the owner decided that if they couldn't come to him, he'd go to them. On-site delivery turned the deli around.

302

Down With Negativity

From Guy Kawasaki

f you believe in your idea, stick to it! Don't let the bozos who have everything to gain by your failure win the head game. People will tell you that your idea will never fly, that you'll never make it, that there's too much competition, that you don't have enough experience. Block out the negativity and be true to your vision.

When a young fellow wanted to start a French bakery in a town loaded with dock workers and roughnecks, people told him he would never make it. But he opened a place that was warm and welcoming, not fancy and fluffy at all. Everyone who went there loved the fabulous food and the relaxed plaid couch and fireplace. The bakery took off and two more are planned to open soon.

303

Love Will Keep Us Together

From Michel Roux

Have fun by doing what you love. It's the surest way to delight customers. If you love what you do, it will show, and your genuine enthusiasm will be infectious. The more excited you are about your business, the more excited your employees and customers will be, too.

One woman loved her panes—stained glass panes, that is. She was nuts about stained glass and after taking a number of classes, she opened her own supply shop and gallery. Her enthusiasm was contagious—soon enough, she had plenty of customers and commissions.

Index

Index Of Marketing Experts

1.

Improve your business.

2.

See the latest trends.

3.

Download free/trial software.

4.

Learn to increase income.

5.

Find your dream business.

6.

Network with your peers.

FREE ADVICE

When was the last time you got **free** advice that was worth something?

<u>Entrepreneur Magazine,</u> the leading small business authority, is loaded with <u>free advice</u>—advice that could be worth millions to you. Every issue gives you detailed, practical knowledge on how <u>to start a business</u> and run it successfully. Entrepreneur is the perfect resource to keep small business owners up-to-date, on track, and growing their business.

BREAK OUT

Business Start-Ups helps you **break** out of the 9–5 life!

<u>Do you want</u> to get out of the 9–5 routine and take control of your life? <u>Business Start-Ups</u> shows you the franchise and business opportunities that will give you the future you dream of. Every issue answers your questions, <u>highlights hot trends,</u> spotlights new ideas, and provides the inspiration and real-life information you need to succeed.

MILLION DOLLAR SECRETS

Exercise your right to make it **big.**

Get into the small business authority—
now at **80% off** the newsstand price!

Yes! Start my one year subscription and
bill me for just $9.99. I get a full year of Entrepreneur
and save 80% off the newsstand rate. If I choose not
to subscribe, the free issue is mine to keep.

Name ☐ Mr. ☐ Mrs. _____
(please print)

Address _____

City _____ State _____ Zip _____

☐ BILL ME   ☐ PAYMENT ENCLOSED

Guaranteed. Or your money back. Every subscription to Entrepreneur comes with a 100% satisfaction guarantee: your money back whenever you like, for whatever reason, on all unmailed issues! Offer good in U.S. and possessions only. Please allow 4–6 weeks for mailing of first issue. Canadian and foreign: $39.97. U.S. funds only.

5G9J9

Mail this coupon to **Entrepreneur** MAGAZINE P.O. Box 50368, Boulder, CO 80321-0368

OPPORTUNITY KNOCKS!!!

save 72%!

Please enter my subscription to Business
Start-Ups for one year. I will receive 12 issues for
only $9.99. That's a savings of 72% off the newsstand
price. The free issue is mine to keep, even if I choose
not to subscribe.

Name ☐ Mr. ☐ Mrs. _____
(please print)

Address _____

City _____ State _____ Zip _____

☐ BILL ME   ☐ PAYMENT ENCLOSED

Guaranteed. Or your money back. Every subscription to Business Start-Ups comes with a 100% satisfaction guarantee: your money back whenever you like, for whatever reason, on all unmailed issues! Offer good in U.S. and possessions only. Please allow 4–6 weeks for mailing of first issue. Canadian and foreign: $34.97. U.S. funds only.

5HBK2

Mail this coupon to **Business Start-Ups** P.O. Box 50347, Boulder, CO 80321-0347